SEXUAL HARASSMENT
Threat to Working Women

SEXUAL HARASSMENT
Threat to Working Women

DR. REENA CHAUDHARY

DEEP & DEEP PUBLICATIONS PVT. LTD.
F-159, Rajouri Garden, New Delhi - 110 027

SEXUAL HARASSMENT
Threat to Working Women

ISBN 978-81-8450-349-4

Typeset by RAHUL COMPOSERS
358, Pocket-B, Phase-2, Sector-16B, Dwarka, New Delhi - 110 075

Printed in India at MAYUR ENTERPRISES
WZ Plot No. 3, Gujjar Market, Tihar Village, New Delhi - 110 018

Published by DEEP & DEEP PUBLICATIONS PVT. LTD.
F-159, Rajouri Garden, New Delhi - 110 027 • Phone : 25435369, 25440916
E-mail : ddpubs@gmail.com • ddpbooks@yahoo.co.in
Showroom :
2/13, Ansari Road, Daryaganj, New Delhi - 110 002 • Telefax : 23245122

Contents

Preface

The literature clearly shows that work is divided into two main categories—'productive' and 'non-productive'. The productive work is most of the time performed by men, whereas the non-productive work is associated with women. However, the world of work is changing, often drastically, due to the move towards a global economy characterized by greater openness or liberalization of markets, free or greater mobility of financial capital and people, and rapid distribution of products, information, technology, and consumption patterns. New risks and opportunities emerged with the globalization of the economy, all of which have different repercussions for female and male workers. The available data indicates that women's economic activity rates and share of the labour force have been increasing in most regions of the world in recent decades. A large number of women have started working outside their homes, many a times in the male dominated occupation which is altogether a naive world for them. The increasing presence of women in paid work and their greater share of employment do not mean that gender inequality has disappeared. Men who consider workplace to be their domain are more dominating at work and keep on discriminating women on many grounds, i.e. wages, promotions, increments, etc. and within the family, these women are likely to remain responsible for childcare and domestic labour, creating a significant double burden. Consequently, male dominance continues to be the rule and they make lewd remarks to make women feel vulnerable at workplace. Furthermore, men are socialized into roles of sexual assertion whereas women are socialized to be passive, submissive and tolerant. These socio-cultural roles are played out at the workplace and women do not report the cases and sexual harassment is the result which explores the myth that educated women are safe. The major objectives of this research are to know the incidence of the problem and to know the coping mechanisms used by women to cope up with the problem.

The Constitution of India talks about equality in Articles 15 and 16 and has also introduced the Sexual Harassment Prevention and Redressal Bill (2004), but how many organizations truly implement sexual harassment policy at workplace. The law prohibits sexual harassment at the workplace but it requires that organizations should develop and publish procedures for reporting and resolving harassment as well as other discrimination issues. It is the time when Government, perpetrators and victims should be aware of it. Policy-makers should awake the slumbers otherwise the rate will go high as well as strict vigilant norms should be there to curb the problem at its initial stage.

The book has been organized into six chapters. The first chapter provides general understanding of the problem of sexual harassment at workplace. To make my work clear, understandable and authentic, I have drawn long references discussing incidence of the problem, characteristics of the victims and perpetrators, consequences and many more. This chapter also focuses on Research Methodology explaining the objectives, sampling and techniques of data collection.

The second chapter focuses on the demographic, socio-economic and family background of the working women. The third chapter titled 'Work Environment' has been divided into two sections. Section I discusses the working environment under which women work and section II discusses their work relationships with their male subordinates, colleagues and superordinates. The fourth chapter titled 'Sexual Harassment' highlights incidence of the problem, reasons for its existence and many more.

I have also taken 10 case studies of women who have been victims of sexual harassment to get in-depth knowledge about the problem which have been discussed in fifth chapter titled 'Case Studies and Analysis'. The sixth chapter on 'Conclusion' focuses on the main findings of the study. In this chapter I have also managed to distil from literature, the essential features, which are related to the present findings. At the end of the book, some Appendices are also given to provide relevant information, including the Interview Schedule.

REENA CHAUDHARY

Acknowledgements

Hereby, I see an opportunity to express my deep sense of gratitude to a number of people who helped me in carrying out the research reported in this book. To begin with, I wish to thank **Dr. Madhurima Mahajan**, Reader, Department of Correspondence Studies, Panjab University, for her invaluable advises and suggestions. She was one who gave me confidence to recognize that it was possible to take such a challenging study. Without her consistent encouragement and guidance this work would have not been possible.

I am really indebted to Dr. (Mrs.) Rajesh Gill, Chairperson, Department of Sociology for her inspirational support and excellent suggestions to improve the quality of my research.

For the development and completion of my book I also feel a deep sense of gratitude:

- to Mr. Arvind Thakur (Lawyer, Punjab and Haryana High Court) who helped me in getting case studies of sexually harassed women;
- to Mr. Rajan Walia (Journalist, *Indian Express*) for his ever available co-operation and introducing me to women who faced sexual harassment;
- to Mrs. Kalra, Librarian, Department of Sociology and Mr. Satish Kumar, Scientist, CSIO, Chandigarh, who always helped me to get latest references, journals, books and other study material;

- to all my respondents and head of the workplaces who allowed me to carry out my research;
- to Mr. G.S. Bhatia of Deep and Deep Publications (P) Ltd. for publishing this book;
- to my friend **Simmi**, for helping and encouraging me throughout the course of my study;
- to my parents; father **Mr. Krishan Garg,** mother **Mrs. Kusum Garg** for encouragement and constant demonstration of love;
- to my in-laws especially my mother-in-law **Mrs. Savitri** and my brother-in-law **Mr. Kuldeep,** who constantly encouraged and helped me out of the way to complete my research. Their level of support is truly uncommon;
- to my beloved husband **Sanjiv Chaudhary** for convincing me to work on this sensitive issue, constant motivation and synergistic support throughout the completion of this book; and
- Finally, but not the least to my daughter **'Ipsita'** for her unprecedented support throughout the work, as she at such a tender age managed herself unattended most of the time.

REENA CHAUDHARY

1

Introduction

Sexual harassment has been practiced since the advent of waged labour, however, it has only been in recent years that women have had a name for their experiences of it. Since then a small number of researchers have started exploring the topic of sexual harassment. It was in the decades of seventies that the phrase sexual harassment was first used. In India, it was the ruling of the Supreme Court (1997) in the famous Vishaka Case that brought the issue to the public consciousness. Sexual harassment at work place in India is 'quite prevalent' but the victims refrain from lodging a complaint facing social disgrace and loss of work. Sexual harassment affects all women in some form or the other. Lewd remarks, touching, wolf-whistles looks are part of any woman's life so much so that it is dismissed as normal. Working women are no exception. In fact, working women most commonly face the backlash to women taking new roles, which belong to male domains within patriarchy. Sexual harassment of working women is an extension of violence in everyday life and is discriminatory, exploitative, thriving in atmosphere of threat, terror and reprisal. The reason for selecting sexual harassment of women at workplace as a topic of research is that in India the research is at its initial stage. Social Scientists are trying to explore the incidence and reasons for its existence. The empirical reality highlights the declining status of women in India, the sex selective abortions and higher rate of crime against women act as a testimony to this fact. Even though a large number of women have started working outside their homes, many a times in the male dominated occupations, the question of their security has gained utmost importance. In order to highlight the hazards of occupations women face, it becomes necessary to take up such problem which clearly refers towards the working women. Keeping these points in mind the present study has been undertaken.

DEFINITIONS OF SEXUAL HARASSMENT

Definitions of sexual harassment vary considerably in different countries, societies, communities and organizations. The term 'sexual harassment' was first used in the 1970s. Since then the issue of sexual harassment has gradually emerged as a recognized phenomenon throughout the world in all cultural and occupational contexts.

International Labour Organization (2001) considers sexual harassment as a violation of fundamental rights of workers, declaring that it constitute a problem of safety and health, a problem of discrimination, an unacceptable working condition and a form of violence, usually against women workers.

U.S. Equal Employment Opportunity Commission (1999) defines sexual harassment as any form of uninvited sexual attention that either explicitly or implicitly becomes a condition of one's work.

The European Commissions (EC) code of practice defines sexual harassment as conduct affecting the dignity of women and men at work. "Sexual harassment means unwanted conduct of a sexual nature, or other conduct based on sex affecting the dignity of women and men at work. This includes unwelcome physical, verbal or non-verbal conduct".

According to Czech Republic, Sexual harassment refers to as undesirable behaviour of a sexual nature at the workplace if such conduct is unwelcome, unsuitable or insulting, or if it can be justifiably perceived by the party concerned as a condition for decisions affecting the exercise of rights and obligations ensuring from labour relations.

Additionally Social Scientists have defined sexual harassment differently. In the approximately 30 years since the term came into being, it has defined as behaviour ranging from sexist jokes to rape. Farley (1978) defined 'Sexual harassment as unsolicited non-reciprocal male behaviour asserting a woman sex role over her function as a worker'.

Stanko (1988) defined sexual harassment as "Unwanted sexual attention". It's behavioural forms are many and include visual (leering); verbal (sexual teasing, jokes, comments on questions); unwanted pressures for sexual favours with implied threats of job-related consequences for non-cooperation; physical assault; sexual assault; rape".

Fitzgerald, one of the foremost researchers of sexual harassment and her colleagues defined sexual harassment psychologically as, "an unwanted sex-related behaviour at work that is appraised by the recipient as offensive, exceeding her resources, or threatening her well-being" (Fitzgerald *et. al.*, 1997).

In Sociology, most scholarly definitions of sexual harassment specify conduct that is "unwelcome or unsolicited, is sexual in nature, and is deliberate or repeated" (Barr, 1993).

Feminist theorists view sexual harassment as the product of a gender system maintained by a dominant, normative form of masculinity. According to Bularzik (1978), the license to harass women workers, which many men feel they have, stems from notions that there is a 'woman's place' which women in the labour force have left, thus leaving behind their 'personal integrity'. According to her, it is the patriarchal norms responsible for her harassment.

From the above definitions, a few points can be deduced. First, sexual harassment at workplace refers to the fact that a person is working for wages that can be temporary or permanent in nature. Second, although sexual harassment is a form of gender violence, but the focus is on female's sexual exploitation at workplace, it does not, however, mean the men are not sexually exploited at workplace. For the present study, however, the focus is kept on female sexual exploitation at workplace. Another point which comes out of these definitions is that harassment results in unwanted or unwelcome gestures by the employee which makes the worker uncomfortable.

SEXUAL HARASSMENT IN THE INDIAN SET-UP

In India, the Supreme Court has defined sexual harassment as:

- Physical contact
- A demand or request for sexual favours
- Sexually coloured remarks
- Showing pornography

Sexual harassment takes place if a person:

- Subjects another person to an unwelcome act of physical intimacy, like grabbing, brushing, touching, pinching, etc.
- Makes an unwelcome demand or request (whether directly or by implication) for sexual favours from another person, and further makes it a condition for employment/payment of wages/increment promotion, etc.
- Makes an unwelcome remark with sexual connotations, like sexually explicit compliments/ cracking loud jokes with sexual connotations/ making sexist remarks, etc.
- Shows a person any sexually explicit visual material, in the form of pictures/cartoons/pin-ups/calendars/ screen savers on computers/any offensive written material/pornographic e-mails, etc.
- Engages in any other unwelcome conduct of a sexual nature, which could be verbal, or even non-verbal, like staring to make the other person uncomfortable, making offensive gestures, kissing sounds, etc.

It is sexual harassment if a supervisor requests sexual favours from a junior in return for promotion or other benefits or threatens to sack for non-co-operation. It is also sexual harassment for a boss to make intrusive inquiries into the private lives of employees, or persistently ask them out. It is sexual harassment for a group of workers to joke and snigger amongst themselves about sexual conduct in an attempt to humiliate or embarrass another person.

Sexual harassment at workplace is generally classified into two distinct types—

- 'Quid pro quo', means seeking sexual favours or advances in exchange for work benefits and it occurs when consent to sexually explicit behaviour or speech is made a condition for employment or refusal to comply with a 'request' is met with retaliatory action such as dismissal, demotion, difficult work conditions.
- 'Hostile working environment' is more pervasive form of sexual harassment involving work conditions or behaviour that make the work environment 'hostile' for the woman to be in. Certain sexist remarks, display of pornography or sexist/obscene graffiti, physical contact/brushing against female employees are some examples of hostile work environment, which are not the conditions of employment. Unwelcome is the key in defining sexual harassment. It is the impact and effect the behaviour has on the recipient that will define the behaviour as sexual harassment.

According to the Supreme Court ruling workplace is any place where working relationships exist, where employer and employee relations exist. The guidelines apply to both organized and unorganized work sectors and to all women whether working part time, on contract or in voluntary/ honorary capacity.

A large number of countries worldwide have adopted some form of legislation on sexual harassment, either by addressing it under another broader statute such as human rights, or equal opportunity and treatment like in non-discrimination, labour, contract, personal injury and criminal laws. In several countries the judiciary has taken the lead in prohibiting sexual harassment, for example, in Denmark,

Greece, Hong Kong SAR, India, Japan, United Kingdom and the United States. In other countries draft, laws and bills are under discussion. There is reluctance in some countries to move too quickly on the adoption of specific legislation. Some believe that legal protection will lead to workplace tensions while others consider voluntary initiatives to be sufficient and, indeed the preferred approach.

FORMULATION OF THE PROBLEM

Work can be divided into two main categories 'productive' and 'non-productive'. In Parsons' terminology we talk about expressive and instrumental roles. Instrumental role goes with productive work which is most of the time performed by men, whereas expressive roles are not considered productive, and they are associated with women.

There is a large evidence to indicate poor, rural women in India have long been involved in subsistence farming within the family. Their unpaid work on the family farm has been and continues to be essential for the subsistence food production. Even in urban areas, poor women are always involved in domestic service. However, the changing scenario has brought a large number of educated upper and middle class women at the workplace. Women have been going out to work outside the home in ever-greater numbers over the past 20 years, to earn income. Many women, however, have to cope with extra strains at work where they are vulnerable to unwanted kinds of attention because they are women.

Women's participation in the labour market has been structured around the assumption that the women are economically dependent on men, and thus do not need a family wage. Women's work is often assumed to be temporary; as young, unmarried women will work until such time as they are married, a supplement to the incomes of male family members. Women's participation in the labour market has been further shaped by the idea that women's skills are analogous to the skills they perform without financial compensation in the family.

Among the poor and working class, women are likely to be engaged in low paying wage labour in the unorganised sector. Within the family, these women are likely to remain responsible for childcare and domestic labour, creating a significant double burden. Among the upper classes, women are more likely to participate in higher paid employment, including professional employment, and to delegate their responsibility for child care and domestic servants employed within the household. Even at the upper income levels in which women may participate in professional occupations, their roles and responsibilities within the family continue to be influenced by the sexual division of labour (Bardhan, 1985). Within dominant normative visions, child care and domestic labour continues to be seen as primarily women's responsibility regardless of nature of their participation in the labour force.

New risks and opportunities have also emerged with the globalization of the economy and with changes in technology and the labour market, all of which have had different repercussions for female and male workers. The available data indicates that women's economic activity rates and share of the labour force have been increasing in most regions of the world in recent decades. However, the gap between men and women continued, with 49.1 percent of women working as employed in 2007 and 74.3 percent of men. The increasing presence of women in paid work and their greater share of employment do not mean that gender inequality has disappeared. These women gain employment but are mostly concentrated in poorly paid or unskilled jobs, characterized by the absence of upward mobility and opportunity. This is most commonly the result of negative or obstructive attitudes and of legal and social systems which use maternity laws and benefits to penalize women economically for child birth and child care responsibilities and discourage or actively prevent men from sharing family responsibilities.

These women face inhospitable environment at workplace. Equality of opportunity and treatment between men and women in the world of work thus remains an important problem. It has led to many evils such as gender discrimination, physical and mental harassment and more specifically sexual harassment at the workplace. Indeed sexual harassment apart from being a dehumanizing act is an unlawful intrusion on the right of privacy and sanctity of a female. It is serious blow to her supreme honour and offends her self-esteem and dignity. It degrades and humiliates the victim particularly where the victim is a helpless innocent.

The issue of sexual harassment is sensitive and difficult to address. When it occurs at the workplace it is not so much a product of the working environment as it is a reflection of traditional social behaviour between the sexes and of social attitudes towards women. Sexual harassment is not confined to the world of work but workers (women) are specifically vulnerable because their families' livelihood is at stake. It is extremely difficult for victims to complain about it without making their situation worse or for fear of losing their jobs. This is because sexual harassment at the work place is treated as "personal" problem between those involved rather than social issue.

Sexual harassment as such has far reaching consequences to the victims, to the victim's family, to the organization, to other employees who witness harassment and more importantly to the society. Victims may develop significant emotional, adjustmental and interpersonal and job-related problems. Sexual harassment has negative repercussions for the companies as they may loose good employees, suffer losses due to de-motivated employees which can further damage image of the work place.

Furthermore, the absence or the inadequate empirical studies carried out on 'sexual harassment at work place' in this region reflects the continuing obfuscation and erasure of the subject. From research perspective it is clear that quantitative and qualitative studies are necessary to elicit data required to stimulate people to prevent and redress the sexual harassment of women.

Thus in carrying out this study it is anticipated that the research findings would provide effective stimulus and data base for appropriate action in this regard by the relevant parties in the future.

UNDERSTANDING SEXUAL HARASSMENT

Sexual harassment is a clear form of gender

discrimination based on sex. The problem of sexual harassment relates not so much to the actual biological differences between men and women, but to the gender or social roles, which are attributed to men and women in social and economic life, and perceptions about male and female sexuality in society. For meaningful discussions on sexual harassment, it is important to keep in mind that gender relations are a social construct. Women, through the centuries in many parts of the world, have been perceived to be, and therefore are socially conditioned from an early age to be subordinate to men. Women are expected to be complainant and sexually passive and men are socialized to believe that they are the ones to initiate sexual relationships and that is reasonable, tolerated or even expected of them to be sexually aggressive.

Inequalities in the position of men and women exist in nearly all societies and sexual harassment at work is a clear manifestation of unequal power relations. Women are much more likely to be victims of sexual harassment precisely because they lack power, are in more vulnerable and insecure positions, lack self-confidence and/or have been socialized that they are to suffer in silence. Women can also become targets of sexual harassment when they are seen to be competing for power or take on new roles. In many societies and situations men are more likely to harass the women as they are often placed in more senior or better-paid positions. Thus, gender inequalities operate within the large matrix of structural inequalities. The implications of such unequal power relations on various aspects of women's life need to be highlighted in the analysis of problems of working women.

STUDIES ON SEXUAL HARASSMENT

Until recently the pervasive problem of sexual harassment has largely been neglected by the researchers. Much of the initial research was essentially descriptive, in that it was aimed at identifying frequency of occurrence, who harasses, who are the victims, the circumstances under which it occurs.

Sexual harassment at workplace affects millions of women around the world regardless of their profession. Sexual favours rather than merit and hard work often remain the determinants of a woman's professional career in a male dominated workplace. The phenomenon of harassment and violence at the workplace is receiving increasing attention, especially in the context of women's rising rates of participation in the labour force and enhanced legal and regulatory provisions.

Keeping in mind different research studies review of literature has been divided into sub-headings like incidence, gender basis of sexual harassment, precipitating factors for the victims and perpetrators, perceptions, consequences, coping mechanism and prevention.

Incidence

It is indisputable that sexual harassment is not an occasional occurrence, but on the contrary, appears to occur in virtually all workplaces to a varying degree.

European Surveys have shown significant rates of sexual harassment at the workplace with between 40 and 50 percent of women in the European Union reporting some form of harassment or unwanted sexual behaviour at the workplace (ILO Report, 2001). During the period 1987-97, 75 research projects have been carried out in 11 European countries, i.e. Austria, Belgium, Denmark, Finland, Germany, Ireland, Luxembourg, Netherlands, Norway, Sweden and the United Kingdom and information on incidence of sexual harassment is collected. The highest incidences rates are found in the national surveys carried out in Austria, Germany and Luxembourg. The Austrian and Luxembourg surveys report a rate of 80 percent and the German research show that 72 percent of employees have been confronted with sexual harassment. In the national Dutch, Finnish and U.K. Studies a somewhat lower incidence figure is reported by female employees: 32 percent, 27 percent and 54 percent. In Sweden, the rate of sexual harassment is lowest at 2 percent (ILO Report, 2001).

In Japan, a large scale survey has been conducted by the Ministry of Labour on 6762 workers and supervisors. Almost 2/3rd of the 2254 women respondents have been sexually harassed at least once (Yamakawa, 2001). In the Republic of

Korea, a survey conducted by the Korean Institute of Criminology finds that 64 percent of the women have been subjected to verbal harassment, 35 percent have reported physical harassment, 34 percent have experienced visual harassment and 25 percent have been forced to attend to men at dinner parties (Zaitun, 2001).

In a survey conducted in Philippines, working women organization reports that out of a total of 43 unionized and 291 non-unionized establishments, 17 percent have records of sexual harassment cases. Of this number, 11 are unionized establishments and 46 are non-unionized thing (Ursua, 2000).

In a survey of two Government departments in Penang and Perlis, the two Northern States of Malaysia, 83 percent and 88 percent of the women respondents respectively have experienced some form of sexual harassment (Peterson, 2000).

In a study by the Human Rights Commission in New Zealand that have reviewed 284 sexual harassment complaints during the period between 1995-2000, it has been found that 90 percent of complaints involve men sexually harassing women. 'Male to Male' harassment is the next most common complaint (6 percent) while 'Female to Female' harassment accounted for 2 percent of the complaints. Fewer than 2 percent of the cases involve women sexually harassing men.

The United States Merit Protection Board (1980, 1987 and 1994) has conducted surveys of federal employees to assess the frequency of sexually harassing behaviour in the non-military federal workplace. In each of these studies, approximately 1/3rd of the female employees report being the target of unwelcome sexual remarks and suggestive looks, 1/4th report physical touching by a co-worker or supervisor. 1/6th report being pressured for dates and 1/10th for sexual favours. 1 percent has experienced rape by co-workers.

In Tanzania, a survey of 10,319 women in 135 workplaces from 13 regions in 1988-89 it has been found that sexual harassment is a common problem affecting women workers. 60 percent of the women indicate that sexual harassment occur at their workplace and is so common that they do not report it (ILO, 1993).

In Bangladesh, a survey of health and safety regulations in the garment industry found that sexual harassment is likely to be the most dominant source of stress for garment workers (Huda, 2001). Another survey by the Bangladesh Institute of Labour Studies (BILS), based on news reports in 12 national dailies, reveals that at least 51 women working in the industrial and service sectors are raped in the first six months of their job. Rape is only the most extreme form of sexual harassment; its frequency is an index of generalized attitudes of hostility towards the harassment of women workers. Statistics drawn from newspapers only capture those incidents that have been reported officially. One can assume that there is a considerable under-reporting of such incidents.

Incidence of Sexual Harassment in India

In 2004, there were 10,001 cases of sexual harassment according to Government of India. In 2006, there were 9966 cases of sexual harassment according to NCRB, India. Andhra Pradesh recorded highest cases of sexual harassment in the country. In India very few studies have been done in this area.

Awag, a women action group, based at Ahmedabad reports on the basis of a survey that about 48 percent of women experience sexually inappropriate behaviour at workplace. The nature of harassment include verbal, psychological and physical. The perpetrators of harassment are usually co-workers or immediate superiors (*Hindustan Times*, 2004).

Srinivasan (1992), reports sexual harassment as one of the problems of the women working in the Banks faced. 50 percent of the respondents complained of sexual harassment from their customers than colleagues. A study conducted by Lal Bahadur Shastri Institute in 2000 has found that 21.4 percent of women civil servants feel sexual harassment is on the increase in premier Government jobs (Kumar, 2007). In a survey conducted by the National Commission reports that 46.5 percent of women report sexual harassment at the workplace; only about 3.5 percent report the matter to authorities; 1.4 percent report it to the police (Srivastava, 2004).

A study of indigenous women labourers in Bihar, India, describes the sexual exploitation of these women by their employers, contractors and co-workers as the greatest humiliation that these women are subjected to as a consequence of their extremely exploitative working conditions and lack of bargaining power. Rape and sexual abuse are common. Frequently the women are held in bondage and if they manage to escape it is not always possible to go back to their villages. Many end up in prostitution or just disappear altogether (Prasad, 1988).

In 2001, a five state survey of working women has been conducted by Sakshi, a Delhi-based NGO. 80 percent of respondents have revealed that sexual harassment exists, 49 percent have encountered sexual harassment, 41 percent have experienced sexual harassment, 53 percent women and men do not have equal opportunities, 53 percent are treated unfairly by supervisors, employers and co-workers, 58 percent have not heard of the Supreme Court's directive of 1997 and only 20 percent of the organizations have implemented the Vishakha guidelines (Dalal, 2003).

An exploratory study has been undertaken in 2005-06 among 135 women health workers, including doctors, nurses, health care attendants, administrative and other non-medical staff working in two Governments and two private hospitals in Kolkata. Four types of experiences are reported by the 77 women who have experienced 128 incidents of sexual harassment: verbal harassment (41), psychological harassment (45), sexual gestures and exposure (15) and unwanted touch (27). None of the women have reported rape, attempted rape or forced sex but number of them knew of other women health workers who have experienced these. The women who have experienced harassment are reluctant to complain, fearing for their jobs or being stigmatized and most are not aware of formal channels for redress. Experiences of sexual harassment reflect the obstacles posed by power imbalances and gender norms in empowering women to make a formal complaint, on the one hand, and receive redress on the other (Chaudhuri, 2007).

Harassment by Whom?

Sexual harassment is typically perpetuated by a person in a position of authority. In a study done it has been indicated that 90 percent of women are harassed by their superior, 7 percent by fellow workers and 3 percent by subordinates (Zaitun, 2001).

Cleveland and Kurst (1993) posited that sexual harassment of workers by their colleagues is the most prevalent form of harassment, yet in these situations formal power or authority differences are not present. However, there are still societal differences due to the value given to the male role and may attempt to gain power or devalue women through subtle forms of sexual harassment such as gender harassment. The fact that women workers are also harassed by fellow workers and subordinates highlights that it is not just power in the workplace that is at play. Gender subordinates of women in society also mean that even women in positions of power can be seen and treated as 'second' by equal or lower ranking workers.

Gender-basis of Sexual Harassment

The majority of sexual harassment studies have focused on male harassers and female targets (Marks and Nelson, 1993; Pryor and McKinney, 1995). Although male to female is the most common form of sexual harassment, other forms do occur. Men are also targets of sexual harassment, as evidenced by the fact that 12 percent (1,843) of the claims filed with the Equal Employment Opportunity Commission (EEOC) have been filed by men (EEOC, 1998). Reports of men being subject to harassment and the number of complaints and legal actions brought by them have increased in recent years. It has been suggested that the most vulnerable groups in the labour force target young men, gay men, members of ethnic or racial minorities and men working in female dominated work groups (Rubenstein, 1992).

Studies have found that female harassers are viewed more positively than male harassers (Baird *et. al.*, 1995; Gutek *et. al.*, 1983). Other studies have found no difference between male and female harassers in a wider variety of sexual behaviours (e.g. sexual coercion).

Perception of Sexual Harassment

Different research studies have tried to focus on perceptions of men and women on the concept of a sexual harassment. Gutek (1995); Lengnick-Hall (1995) mention that male and female often differed in their perceptions of what is and what is not sexual harassment.

Stockdale *et. al.* (1995) finds that harassed women are almost four times likely to acknowledge their experiences as sexual harassment than men.

Gutek and O'Connor (1995) conclude that women as compared to men are generally more liberal, broad and inclusive in their definition of sexual harassment. Women perceive a broader range of behaviour as offensive (Rotundo *et. al.*, 2001) and report harassment at higher levels than men (Magley *et. al.*, 1992). Although some researchers have shown that women and men experience sexual harassment equally (Rospenda *et. al.*, 2000).

A few researchers state that the perceptions of men and women not only differed but women's perceptions of sexual harassment also varied with age. Older women find physical touch unacceptable while the younger women are less formal in their social interactions with male colleagues. Concerns voiced by women in China included younger women being coerced or encouraged to subtly exploit their looks, for example, to clinch a deal or enable hotel guests to have a good time (The Lawyers' Collective, 2001 and Tang, 2000). In another study it is indicated that while older women tend to put up with sexual harassment, younger generations of women show resistance to sexual harassment practices because of increased awareness and the need to assert a sense of self-dignity (Wijayatilake and Zackariya, 2000).

There is theoretical and empirical support for the principle that women are more threatened by their perpetrators who are often men (EEOC, 1980) and who have greater social status and power compared to women (Cleveland & Kurst, 1993). Therefore, women may be harmed by sexual harassment more than men. Women more frequently experience these behaviours (Bjorkquist *et. al.*, 1994) and in more chronic forms (Rospenda *et. al.*, 2000) compared to men. Gender alone may not be the reason for perception differences between females and males. Instead, gender differences may mask the underlying influence of sensitivity to sexual harassment as the best predictor of perceptual differences

(Blakely, *et. al.*, 1995; Konard and Gutek, 1986). Several researchers have suggested that characteristics of the victims (age, sex, occupational status, marital status, and ethnicity) influence the perception of sexual harassment (Fain and Anderton, 1987; Gutek, 1985; U.S. Merit Systems Protection Board, 1981, 1988).

Work Environment

The amount of risk a woman assumes varies according to the type of environment in which she performs her work. Women who work in highly sexualized environments are likely to experience more harassment (Loe, 1996). It has also been suggested that sexual harassment occur more frequently in organizations with highly skewed sex ratio because women are forced into more frequent contact with men in such organizations (Gutek *et. al.*, 1990). Sexualized environments have also been shown to create atmosphere that encourage more serious and direct sexual harassment. When obscenities are common in the work place women are three times more likely to be treated as sex objects and be directly sexually harassed than in environments where profanity is not tolerated and when sexual joking is common, sexual harassment is three to seven times more likely to occur (Boland, 2002).

Fitzgerald & Shullman (1993); O'Connell & Korabik (2000) have pointed out that lack of formal policies and enforcement concerned with sexual harassment encourage such behaviours. Bowes-Sperry *et. al.* (2002), Lach & Gwartney— Gibbs (1993), Sbraga & O'Donohue (2000), and Hulin, *et. al.* (1996) have proposed that sexual harassment is less likely to occur in organizational settings that are not tolerant of it.

Those who work in male-dominated workplaces or who assume masculine occupations report more harassment than those who perform jobs associated with women's work (Gruber, 1998). Especially vulnerable are those who depend on men for job security or career advancement (Defour, 1990).

Chappel & Maritino (2000) report that women in non-traditional jobs and predominantly male environments and women who work for male supervisor's have been found to be more likely to be subjected to harassment. Sexual harassment is more prevalent in places where it is considered normal for men to harass women sexually as part and parcel of every day life. For example, in Republic of Korea, it is a common thinking, "Sexual Harassment is a source of energy for working life" (Zaitun, 2001). In Nepal, one in ten of male respondents feel that sexual harassment is a simple harmless flirt that brightens the atmosphere in the workplace (Pradhan-Mala, 2001).

Majority of jobs in military continue to be viewed as "men's work". As the number of women inside military academics and on the bases has grown, so have the number of sexual harassment complaints (Moss, 1997).

CHARACTERISTICS OF VICTIMS AND PERPETRATORS

Victims

A few researchers have examined the characteristics of the victims in an attempt to establish a profile of high risk individuals.

Merit Systems Protection Board (1981) has found that typical women who are likely to be harassed are young, not married, have a higher education, members of a minority, racial or ethnic group, in trainee positions, in non-traditional positions, supervised by someone of the opposite sex. Chappel & Maritino (2000) have reported similar findings that single, separated, widowed and divorced are at a higher risk of harassment.

The General Union of workers in Spain has found that women between 26 and 30 years old are more likely to be harassed than any other age groups. Women who are separated, divorced or widowed not only more likely to be subject to sexual harassment, but they also experience stronger forms of harassment (Fuentes, 1988). A survey of Federal employees in the United States has indicated that women are sexually harassed if they are single or divorced, between the ages of 20 and 44, have some university education, have a non-traditional job, or work in a predominantly male environment or for a male supervisor.

Women who are more dependent on men for employment and educational opportunities than others, and as a result, their risk is especially high (Decoster *et. al.,* 1999). Women who depend solely on their wages to support themselves and their families are unlikely to take risk at work. Their reluctance to either confront or complain makes them easy prey for sexual harassment (Stambaugh, 1997).

Mode Market Research Agency has conducted a poll in four major metropolitan cities in India. Results show that 42 percent respondents report that clerical and administrative staff is more likely to be harassed at work, 31 percent of them feel that middle class executives are also at risk. Almost 74 percent of the sample polled feels that several men in superior position take advantage of their positions by making passes at their subordinate women. Women who challenge the superiority of men by acquiring social, economic or organizational power over them are visible targets for sexualized hostility. In fact, the findings from one study have revealed that women who possess more work experience and higher education qualification are at the greater risk of sexual harassment and victimization (Decoster *et. al.,* 1999). Thus the more power a woman acquires, the more she is perceived to be a threat to those in power and the greater her risk of being sexually harassed will be.

It is also apparent that the kind of workplace in which a woman is employed plays a significant factor role in her being harassed. Women in non-traditional jobs and predominantly male environments and women who work for male supervisors are found to be more prone to harassment (European Commission, 1999).

Different researchers have reported that women who work in hospital industry like hospitals, hotels, restaurants, travelling, etc. face harassment not only from employees but also customers. In a study of Airline Industry, Airhostesses report that they are often harassed in the course of their flight, with clients' unnecessary calling for them and asking personal questions such as "Are you married?" Some air travelers apparently ask for specific employees like "send the pretty one". Apart from the harassment itself, the employee also often ends up being ridiculed by her colleagues (Pradhan-Malla, 2001).

Perpetrators

It should be emphasized that all men are not harassers although a demographic profile of the typical harassers is not easy to come by, it is certainly true that some men are much more likely to harass than others.

One of the difficulties in understanding sexual harassment is that it involves a range of behaviour, and is often difficult for the recipient to describe to themselves, and to others, exactly what they are experiencing. Moreover, behaviour and motives vary between individual harassers.

Dzeich & Weiner (1990) has divided harassers into two broad classes:

- Public harassers, are flagrant in their seductive or sexiest attitudes towards colleagues, subordinates, etc.
- Private harassers carefully cultivate a restrained and respectable image on the surface, but when alone with their target, their demeanor changes completely.

Langelan (1993) describes three different classes of harassers:

- Predatory Harassers, who get sexual thrills from humiliating others. This harasser may become involved in sexual extortion, and may frequently harass just to see how targets respond—those who don't resist may even become targets for rape.
- Dominance harassers, who engage in harassing behaviour as an ego boost, it is the most common type.
- Strategic or Territorial harassers, who seek to maintain privilege in jobs or physical locations, for example a man's harassing female employees is a predominantly male occupation.

The women employees report that their harassers are mostly males, married, colleagues and older than the victims. Minority women are more likely to be harassed by a person of a different race or ethnicity (Merit Systems Protection Board, 1981).

However, there are other studies which have found that perpetrators exist in all occupations and social groups and appear to come from all ages and marital statuses indeed it is not possible to identify any particular observable characteristic that is associated with harasser status aside from the simple fact of being male. The majority of sexual harassment studies have focused on male harassers and female targets. But it is also true that there are female harassers and male targets also. Most of the men have reported that their harassers are female, divorced or single, fellow employees and younger to them.

Pryor *et. al.* (1995) have found that male perpetrators are characterized by misogynistic attitudes and hostility towards women, adversarial sexual beliefs and commitment to the traditional role arrangement between the sexes. Harassers are overwhelmingly men. Perpetrators of sexual harassment are mostly colleagues or superiors. Far behind, are patients, clients and finally subordinates.

The Shroud of Silence

Sexual harassment is common problem, but remains hidden behind a wall of silence and ridicule. Victims are ashamed or embarrassed about what happened to them and prefer to keep quite about it, often also because they are afraid of being labeled as either "Loose" women or "Frigid" women who cannot take a joke (Wijayatilake & Zackariya, 2000).

A large number of studies have found that women who report sexual harassment are doubly victimized: first, when they are harassed and subsequently through the protracted and traumatic process of redress, the victim is blamed and stigmatized and her prospects of continuing work is affected (Devika & Kodoth, 2001). Women remain silent from fear of having the event trivialized (Jayashree, 1999; Tejani, 2004) or loosing employment (Chaudhury, 2007; Srivastava, 2004).

Most women first attempt to handle sexual harassment at work by ignoring it and hoping their harasser will desist (Terpstra & Baker, 1991). According to the Working Women United Institute (1975) survey, 75 percent women ignore the behaviour. Women do not complain because they feel that nothing will be done, their claims will be treated lightly, they will be blamed or will suffer some repercussions if they complain, and a feeling of guilt (Di Tomaso, 1991; Gruber & Bjorn, 1986). Srivastava (2004) has given some main causes of non-reporting of sexual harassment, i.e. fear of losing job, fear of not getting promotions, fear of victimization by the employer, fear of being neglected by her family members and among others, slow to improve the situation.

Sandroff (1992) has reported that the vast majority of women who are harassed do not feel that they can safely report the problem. Moreover, women who have complained of harassment are the blamed as troublemakers (Clarke, 1988; Firestone and Harris, 1997; Grauerholz *et. al.*, 1999; Livingston, 1982). Many are afraid of retaliation (Silverman, 1977), or afraid that they will be blamed for the problem (Thacker, 1992). These concerns may be well founded as the consequences of making a complaint are often unfavourable. Specifically, women report that the situation becomes worse after complaining (Livingston, 1982), the complaint is ignored (Sandroff, 1992), the complainant is forced to quit (Coles, 1986; Terpstra & Cook, 1985), or the perpetrator only receives a token reprimand (Riger, 1991; Sandroff, 1992). Researches have found that judgments of a woman complainant adversely influences if the woman is dressed in a provocative and sexy manner (Pryor & Day, 1988), wear too much (Workman & Johnson, 1991), have a feminist orientation (Summers, 1991), competing for career opportunities with the perpetrator (Summers, 1991), engages in self-blame (Valentine-French & Radtke, 1989), or acquires to demands for sexual favours (Hartnett, *et. al.*, 1989).

The type of harassment also effects a victim's decision to respond. *Quid pro quo* harassment is more likely to result in formal complaints, while hostile working environments are more likely to produce informal responses (Harris & Firestone, 1997). Since studies show that environmental harassment is more common than *quid pro quo* harassment, most sexual harassments remains unreported.

Many do not report sexual harassment simply because they do not know how to and whom to seek assistance from. Illiteracy and lack of understanding of information pose difficulties for women working in unorganized sector (ILO, 1997).

One major reason why victims do not respond directly in sexual harassment situations is that they fear retaliation by the harasser. In many cases the victim is in a low power position in an organization, it can jeopardize her position and possibility for advancement if she adopts an assertive coping response to harassing behaviour. Stockdale (1998) has determined that sexual harassment victims experience negative outcomes if they respond to the harassment behaviour in a direct confrontational manner. Coles (1986) has also found that many female employees who initiate a sexual harassment complaint either have to quit their jobs or are fined.

Sexual harassment is not easy to handle, it presents a real threat to economic security and traps women in a role conflict with all its resultant anxiety and stress. Facing the harassment and having to deal with it in public is probably worse than suffering in silence (Watson, 1994).

Consequences

Effects of sexual harassment can vary depending on the individual, the severity and duration of the harassment. However, many situations can have life altering affects particularly when they involve severe/chronic abuses, retaliation against a victim who does not submit to the harassment, who complains about it openly. Indeed, psychologists and social workers have asserted that severe/chronic sexual harassment can have the same psychological effects as sexual assault (Koss, 1987). Backlash and victim-blaming can further aggravate the effects (Boland, 2002). Some sexual harassment effects include, one's personal life opens up for public scrutiny, being humiliated by scrutiny and gossip, defamation of character and reputation, loss of trust in the types of people that occupy similar positions as the harasser.

Gutek & Koss (1993) have noted that negative job-related outcomes such as voluntary quits, transfers and reassignments, terminations, deterioration of interpersonal relationships with co-workers and decrease in job satisfaction and organizational commitment. Danish Gallup Institute (1991); Fitzgerald *et. al.* (1997) mention that women who are harassed report lower levels of job satisfaction and higher levels of absenteeism (Coles, 1986; Crull, 1982). 10 percent of women quit a job because of sexual harassment (U.S. Merit Systems Protection Board, 1981, 1988, 1985; Gutek & Koss, 1993).

Some of the psychological and health effects of sexual harassment include: reduced self-esteem and life satisfaction, stress, anger, fear, depression, anxiety, nervousness, irritability, loss of motivation, sleeplessness, shame and guilt, difficulty in concentrating, headache, fatigue, stomach problems, weight loss, feeling powerless, increased blood pressure, withdrawal and isolation, traumatic stress, post-traumatic stress disorder, suicidal thoughts, jaw tightness, teeth grinding, nausea, crying spells, disruption of sexual adjustment, etc. (Dansky & Kilpatrick, 1997; Fitzgerald *et. al.,* 1997; Glomb *et. al.,* 1999; Gutek, 1985; Livingston, 1982; Stewart & Robinson, 1995). Female employees experience deterioration in their emotional or physical condition as a result of experiencing unwanted sex-related behaviour at work (Crull, 1982; United States Merit Systems Protection Board, 1981, 1987).

Sexual harassment at workplace may lead to companies facing number of set backs, such as loosing good employees, loss of productivity, discontented and unhappy employees, damage to the goodwill of the company, increase in team conflict, decrease in success at meeting financial goals, legal costs if the problem is ignored and complainant take the issue to court (Bennett-Alexander, 1995; Knapp *et. al.,* 1997).

Dansky and Kilpatrick (1997), argue that women who have experienced unwanted sexual attention or sexual coercion at some point during their careers are likely to experience depression and symptoms of post-traumatic stress disorder. Thus, sexual harassment is very common and has far reaching consequences, to the victim, to the company, to the victim's family, to other employees who witness harassment and more important to the society. Victims of sexual harassment may develop significant psychiatric, emotional, behavioural, interpersonal, somatic and job-related pathology and/or dysfunction. Coping with the negative effects of sexual harassment is emotionally distressing as well as physically exhausting. Those who manage to survive the experience gain strength and wisdom from their adversity (Stambaugh, 1997).

For some, the experience of surviving their harassment, complaint, or litigation experience results in a significant increase in personal pride and sense of self-worth.

BLAMING WOMEN FOR SEXUAL HARASSMENT

A number of studies have shown that men blame women for sexual harassment. Women's dress and appearance are often cited as the 'reason' why women are sexually harassed. As a consequence women who have been harassed begin to doubt themselves (Wijaytilake & Zackariya, 2000, Zaitun, 2001). Even when the perpetrator is penalized the public perception that the woman as either the cause of the incident, or that her 'morals' are questionable continue to plaque the victim. In a study, a woman worker who has reported a case of sexual harassment eventually left her position even though the perpetrator has been dealt with. The main reason is the public pressure (Tang, 2000). The view that women 'ask for it' is so deeply entrenched in some cultural contexts and communities that victims of sexual harassment are blamed and 'tainted' for the rest of their lives. A 'woman's chastity' will be questioned once she is involved in something related to sex, even if she is the victim (Tang, 2000).

Sexual Harassment is considered to be the price, which women must pay for having stepped out of the closed spaces segregated for them. The fact that young mostly unmarried women migrate and live and work on their own, away from their families make people instinctively suspicious with regard to their life styles. Such stigmatization further exacerbates the situation (Huda, 2001).

Coping Styles

Fitzgerald & Shullman (1993) have suggested two types of coping styles utilized by sexual harassment victims. One is problem-focused (i.e. external) and other is emotion–focused (i.e. internal) approach of the victim. A problem-focused approach includes avoiding the harasser, confronting or reporting the aggressor or seeking social support from friends and colleagues. An emotion-focused approach involves trivializing the incidents or reconceptualizing the behaviour as friendliness or helpfulness.

On the other hand, a few researchers have reported that victims don't respond assertively. They don't directly confront the harasser as they don't report their harassment to the organization but instead respond passively to the harassment experience (Gruber & Smith, 1995). Studies from the United States and Canada, for example, show that only around 10 to 20 percent of victims report sexual harassment to someone in authority in their organization. Instead, they tend to ignore the harassment, deflect it by treating it as a joke or by going along with it, or attempt to avoid the harasser. Similarly, in studies done in Northern Europe found that most employees responded by ignoring the behaviour asking the perpetrator to stop. They either fear negative consequences for responding in other ways or believe their complaints will not be taken seriously.

Many women say and do nothing about the harassment because they are only too aware of how sexual harassment is popularly perceived and trivialized. They also feel that they may be laughed at or accused as having exaggerated the incident. They either sincerely believe that if they ignore the 'typical male' behaviour will go away (Pradhan-Malla, 2001; Wijayatilake & Zackariye, 2000; Zaitun, 2001).

Studies at workplace harassment and coping show that victims most often manage their experiences by trying to avoid and ignore the offensive behaviours (Grubber & Smith, 1995; Keashly *et. al.*, 1994). Victims also rely on different forms of social support from friends, family and co-workers (Richman, *et. al.*, 2001), including support from more formal associations (e.g. community or religious organizations).

Prevention

The prevention of sexual harassment at the workplace has received considerable attention (Bresler & Thacker, 1993; Kronenberger & Bourke, 1981; Moyanahan, 1993; Thacker, 1992). Efforts to prevent sexual harassment have traditionally focused on the development of organizational sexual harassment policies and education programs for the victims. However, Biaggio, *et. al.* (1990) have noted, effective policies against sexual harassment should not place all of the responsibility on potential victims. Training directed at potential harassers may be an important part of preventing sexual harassment (Biaggio *et. al.,* 1990; Moyanahan, 1993; Pryor, *et. al.,* 1993).

GAPS IN THE LITERATURE

Additionally, hardly any empirical study has been done in this part of the country. A few isolated empirical studies have been done by NGOs who report the incidence and existence of sexual harassment. Most of these studies have not used any theoretical framework to highlight the causes and precipitating factors for the existence of this problem. Review of literature focuses on the fact this problem needs attention, especially in Indian context where research is anecdotal. It is believed that working women don't constitute a homogeneous category. For the present study an attempt was made to study women working in private sector occupations.

THEORETICAL FRAMEWORK

Different researchers who are working in the area of sexual harassment have come out with different theoretical frameworks. Let us discuss some of the main views.

I. Natural/Biological Theory

Those who belong to natural school of thought assert that harassing behaviour is actually natural and inevitable. Men have stronger sex derives, and are therefore, biologically motivated to engage in sexual pursuit of women. To ensure genetic survival, the ideal reproductive strategy for men is to pursue and impregnate as many women as possible. Women are naturally more reticent in socio-sexual situations and more offended by unsolicited sexual interest. The sexes thus have conflicting interests in sexual encounters, a conflict that leads to sexual harassment. According to some researches, the sexual harassment that women experience is a function of their own deficiency or the deficiency of individual men. Either the woman is incapable of handling an overture or she is overly sensitive. A man may be too assertive or unable to properly control his sex drive. This explanation, however, found little support. (Tangri *et. al.*; 1982).

This biological/evolutionary approach has been criticized on a number of grounds; most important, because it can support conflicting predictions, it is not falsifiable and thus not scientific in the accepted sense of the word. In any event, the framework has had little influence on mainstream thinking about sexual harassment.

II. Psychoanalytical Framework

Freudian and neo-freudian theories have analyzed that why certain men use violence against women such as harassment at workplace is mainly due to intrapsychic conflict, personality disorders, denial mechanisms, developmental deficiencies/impaired ego, narcissism, traumatic childhood. According to psychoanalytical explanation, the cause of any type of violence is located primarily inside the person.

Psychoanalytical theories have been criticized for reducing violence to the product of a determined individual personality outside of social relations on even for attributing it the personality of the victim. They are often labeled as anti-women.

III. Power Theory

This perspective emphasizes that the structure of organizational hierarchy invests power in certain individuals over others, power that can, in and of itself, lead to abuse. Men have traditionally held the organizational power inherent in management and supervisory positions, whereas women are likely to be employed in subordinate positions. It is this imbalance of power that leads to sexual imposition on women; in other words, men harass women because they have the opportunity and means to do so. Sexual harassment is all about expression of male power over women that sustain patriarchal relations. It is used to remind women of their vulnerability and subjugated status.

Power theory, although difficult to test directly, is consistent with the empirical data and accounts fairly convincingly for the means and facilitating conditions of harassment; this is particularly the case if motivational factors (e.g., preservation of masculine dominance and male heterosexual privilege) are incorporated. But explanation of the explicitly sexual nature of harassment is missing here.

IV. Social/Cultural Theory

Culturally-based theories don't focus on the power positions of individuals, but rather on the immediate environment of sexual harassment. Social/Cultural theory asserts that women's lesser status in the larger society is reflected at the workplace structures and culture; consequently, male dominance continues to be the rule. Men are naturally reluctant to relinquish this superior position of privilege. Furthermore, men are socialized into roles of sexual assertion, leadership, persistence, whereas women are socialized to be passive, submissive and sexual gatekeepers. These social/cultural roles are played out at the workplace, and sexual harassment is the result. Sexual harassment reflects the larger society's differential distribution of power and status between the sexes.

With the prevalence of patriarchal culture in the society, a woman is perceived as an object of enjoyment. The perpetrators of sexual harassment have no regard for woman as an equal human being. Under the patriarchal culture mauling and molesting women is part and parcel of the male idea of fun.

V. Sex Role Theory

Sex Role theory suggests that social norms and stereotypes about masculinity may result in female harassment of men being perceived as more acceptable than male harassment of women (Collier and Williams, 1981). In our society men are often stereotyped as being receptive to and welcoming of the sexual advances of women. In contrast, women stereotypically are not as receptive to and welcoming of the sexual advances of men (Collier and Williams, 1981). Gutek *et. al.* (1983), found that behaviour initiated by a woman was viewed as "more appropriate, or keeping within the bounds of the work role". It may be, therefore, that when sexual behaviour is described in different gender contexts, participants use these stereotypes in reacting to and evaluating cases. As a result, male-to-female sexual harassment is viewed more negatively than female-to-male sexual harassment because the perceived degree of unwelcomeness of the behaviour is greater in the former case rather than in the later.

VI. Sex Role Spillover Theory

According to Sex Role Spillover Theory (Gutek and Morasch, 1982), sexual harassment is most likely to occur in work environments where the sex ratio is skewed in either direction. In the male dominated work place, a woman's gender is a salient feature because of her singularity and distinctiveness. Thus, women in the male dominated workplace stand out and are perceived in their sex role over and above recognition in their work role. In the female dominated workplace, sex role and work role overlap. However, it fails to include organizational variables other than sex ratio to both the harasser and the victim that may be important factors.

In a society where violence against women, both subtle and direct, is borne out of the patriarchal values operating in society, force women's conformity to gendered roles. These patriarchal values and attitudes of both men and women pose the greatest challenge in resolution and prevention of sexual harassment. As stated earlier sexual harassment is a multidimensional problem, it will be difficult to focus only one theoretical framework to draw conclusions. For the present study power theory, socio-cultural approach and sex role theory in combination will be used to find the existence and causal factors of sexual harassment.

OBJECTIVES

- To find out the profile of the respondents, their work environment and their relationship with male colleagues, superordinates and subordinates at workplace.
- To find out the incidence of the problem, i.e. to what an extent sexual harassment is prevalent among women at work place.

- To explore working women's perception about sexual harassment, whether their understanding of sexual harassment coincides with Supreme Court's definition.
- To find out the main precipitating factors responsible for the problem of sexual harassment keeping in mind different theoretical frameworks namely power theory, socio-cultural approach and sex role theory.
- To uncover and explore the main factors that would affect women's decisions for lodging a complaint in case of sexual harassment e.g. women who are needy or single would hesitate to lodge a complaint.
- To find out the types of coping mechanisms used by women at workplace to handle the problem of sexual harassment.

RESEARCH METHOD

Research is done in order to extend, correct or verify knowledge, whether that knowledge aids in the construction of a theory or in the practice of an art. Since research is a scientific and systematic search, a definite procedure is adopted. Accordingly, there are two basic approaches to research:

- Quantitative Approach
- Qualitative Approach

Quantitative Approach to research is born on the measurement of quantity or amount. It is applicable to phenomenon that can be expressed in terms of quantity. It involves the generation of data in quantitative form, which can be subjected to rigorous quantitative analysis in a formal or rigid fashion.

Qualitative Approach to research is concerned with qualitative phenomenon. It is concerned with subjective assessment of attitudes, opinion and behaviours. This type of research aims at discovering the underlying motives and desires.

For the present study, both qualitative and quantitative approaches were used. 200 women working in the private sector (organized and unorganized) were studied for quantitative analysis and 10 case studies of women who faced sexual harassment at work place were recorded. The idea was to give more depth to the study.

RESEARCH DESIGN

The research design constitutes the blue print for the collection, measurement and analysis of data. For any research, it is very essential to design the research. The design of research is determined by the objectives of research.

Sexual harassment is an upcoming problem; review of literature highlights that very limited research has been done in Indian Context. Thus, research design for the present study is partially exploratory and partially descriptive. It is exploratory in the sense that here an attempt has been made to assess a detailed and in-depth exploratory analysis of women who faced sexual harassment at workplace. At the same time this study is partially descriptive. It helps to relate to the studies conducted by various researchers through quantitative information in different parts of the world.

UNIVERSE AND SAMPLING FRAME

The study has been conducted in the Union Territory of Chandigarh. In Chandigarh, the total number of working women's population according to census 2001 is 16.45 percent. It becomes essential to highlight what type of problems women face at their workplace. Sexual harassment is one such problem, which needs immediate attention. For the purpose of present study, the Supreme Court's definition of sexual harassment has been used. Fitzgerald had developed a framework, i.e. Sexual Experiences Questionnaire for measuring the prevalence of sexually harassing behaviour (SEQ, Fitzgerald, *et. al.* 1995). Adapted from this, a scale referring to different dimensions as mentioned in the definition of the Supreme Court has been developed. Different dimensions included subtle bribes, subtle threats, poor treatment for not submitting to sexual advances, crude sexual remarks, offensive remarks, sexist comments, unwanted sexual attention, staring or leering, repeated request for sexual favours, physical contact such as touching, brushing, etc. and showing or using pornographic materials has been used to assess prevalence of sexual harassment as well as to measure what women saw as sexual harassment. Each of these items has been presented on a five point Likert Scale. These items have been tested to find out respondents interpretations of sexual harassment. For all items cumulative score has been taken out and statements have been arranged in mild and strong type. To know, sexual harassment quartile deviation has been used (see Appendices I through VI). Sexual harassment is rooted in cultural practices and is exacerbated by power relations at the workplace. It is eleven years since the Supreme Court has laid down guidelines to deal with sexual harassment at workplace. However, the guidelines for most parts continue to languish on paper. Apart from public sector bodies, which have been forced by Government resolutions to implement the guidelines, a large number of private organizations and women working in informal sectors are hardly governed by such policy. Keeping such a situation, in mind, through present study an attempt has been made to study women working in private sector through quantitative analysis. It has been discussed in different empirical studies that the fear of loosing the job is the most important issue in the mind of a woman who has to file a complaint. The more the insecurity, greater are chances of underreporting of sexual harassment. The perpetrator is also aware of this weakness of the victim, thus harassment is one form or the other continues for the victim. She remains helpless in such a situation.

Complete coverage of the whole population was impossible due to many constraints such as limitation of necessary resources and time. Further, there is no information available on working women in the private sector. For the present study, a purposive sample of 200 women working in the private sector (includes both organized and unorganized sectors) was drawn. Different research studies have clearly stated that women who have odd working hours, who work in highly sexualized situation, where legislative enforcement is less, where job insecurity is more, chances of harassment are maximum (ILO, 2001). Keeping these facts in mind different occupational groups were covered. Doctors, Administrative Officers, Journalists, Actresses, Nurses, Clerks, Receptionists, Sweepers working in Hospitals, Hotels and various Private Offices, Construction Workers, Factory Workers and Waitresses in Hotels and Restaurants, etc. were included in the present study.

Additionally, 10 case studies of women who have been victims of sexual harassment and worked in different occupations (both government and private) were taken. Snow ball technique has been used to collect these case studies.

TYPES OF DATA

- Primary
- Secondary

The primary data are those, which are collected for the first time and are original in character. In the present study, for collecting primary data, interview schedule and case study method has been used.

Interview Schedule

Sexual harassment is a sensitive issue especially among Indians due to many reasons such as our cultural constrains, it is difficult to get intended accurate information easily. Thus, an interview schedule was constructed to collect relevant information from the working women. Keeping in view the objectives of the study, different open-ended and close-ended questions were formulated. Interview schedule, thus, prepared was pre-tested on 15 respondents. The language of a few questions was redrafted in the light of the comments of the respondents as well as to remove the possibilities of ambiguities. The interview schedule had different sections to elicit information from the respondents. In addition to socio-economic background of the respondents, information was also sought with regard to number of male and female members of the family and their income. Further, questions related to their profession such as age of joining the profession, introducer to the profession, number of work hours, travelling, etc. have been included. To get the information related to that what type of relationship respondents have with their male colleagues, superordinates and subordinates, different statements were formulated, i.e. males treat them equal, males treat them intelligent or inferior, independently can handle their work, males treat them as showpiece in the workplace, etc. Further, questions related to sexual harassment at workplace were formulated. Exploring the topic of sexual harassment at the workplace was a challenging task. For the large majority of women, it was the first time they were formally discussing the issue. In order to establish rapport with the respondents, they were first asked about sexual harassment of other females in their workplace. Later, they were asked about their own experiences of sexual harassment. Keeping in mind all the components of the Supreme Court's definition, i.e. unwelcome remarks, verbal and non-verbal conduct of sexual nature, sexually suggestive visual material, unwelcome demands or requests and physical contacts, respondents were asked to report sexual harassment. The respondents who faced any kind of sexual harassment at workplace, were included among the 'sexual harassment' cases. Further, questions related to reasons for the existence of the problem, punishment for the perpetrators and measures to be taken for checking the problem were formulated. The second section of the interview schedule focused on the definition of sexual harassment given by the Supreme Court. Different statements on various components, i.e. unwelcome remarks, Verbal and non-verbal demands or requests and physical contacts were formulated to understand the perceptions of the women respondents. These statements were further exaggerated to get knowledge about sexual harassment at workplace in a better perspective. This section of the interview schedule was formulated on the basis of five point Likert scale to gather information regarding perception of working women on the definition of sexual harassment given by the Supreme Court.

Case Study Method

The case study method is a very popular form of qualitative analysis as well as an important method of exploratory study. The advantages of case study method are its applicability to real life contemporary human situations and its public accessibility through written reports. The results related directly to the common readers everyday experience and facilitate in understanding complex real life situation. It leads to new insights and presents a true picture of their lives.

For greater understanding of the problem, 10 case histories of women who faced sexual harassment at work place were taken. Each case study was recorded through several meetings with the victim. This technique was used to understand, what kind of sexual harassment cases faced at workplace, at what age faced the problem, who were the harassers, i.e. superordinates, colleagues or subordinates, trauma they faced, coping mechanism adopted by the cases, etc. Further, the qualitative information gathered from the selected cases was also used to check the analysis based on sample data.

The Secondary Data

Secondary data consisted of published and unpublished materials in the form of books, reports, journals, news reports and periodicals and material from Internet. Since there were limited research studies available in the library. Different sites of ILO, UNO and NCW were used for collecting research material.

TABULATION

After collecting all the information, it was transferred into a code design and was entered into the computer. Using the statistical package for social sciences (SPSS), simple frequency and cross tables were made. As the present study is an exploratory study based on purposive sample no test of significance was used.

For 10 case studies, analysis was done. The idea was to bring out the similarities and uniqueness of these cases in the light to objectives of the study undertaken. The whole investigation has been undertaken to examine their own perception of the problem and coping mechanisms. It included their socio-economic background, problem of sexual harassment, characteristics of the perpetrators, trauma faced by the victim, reactions of victims, etc.

After the collected data was analyzed and interpreted, results were related with a number of studies mentioned in the review of literature. An attempt was made to relate quantitative data with qualitative analysis in the light of theoretical framework used.

CHAPTER SCHEME

The *Chapter 1* of the study focuses on Introduction of the problem of sexual harassment of women at workplace. Different research studies and various theoretical frameworks have been discussed in this chapter. Methodology is part of this chapter. The *Chapter 2* of the study deals with the socio-economic background of the respondents. The *Chapter 3* deals with their work environment and discusses relationship of the respondents with male colleagues, superordinates and subordinates. *Chapter 4* deals with the sexual harassment of women at workplace. It focuses on the incidents and perceptions of working women in relation to the definition of sexual harassment formulated by the Supreme Court. This chapter also discusses the reasons, punishment, measures, etc. related to the problem of sexual harassment. The *Chapter 5* deals with the in-depth study of the 10 cases that faced sexual harassment at workplace and analysis of these case studies. *Chapter 6* deals with summary and conclusion of the study.

2

Socio-Economic and Family Background of Working Women

Individual's birth in a particular family, region and religious faith not only determines his/her life opportunities but also provides him/her with a specific outlook towards life to face social reality. The factors, which influence lifestyle, can broadly be divided into two categories: ascribed and achieved. The former includes the family background, kinship, caste, religion, etc. and the later includes an individual's education, occupational skills, economic position, the friendship circle, the type of the house, the locality in which he/she lives, etc. Both these factors are important to understand the background of the respondents.

The present chapter seeks to analyze the demographic, socio-economic and family background of the respondents. These variables play a very distinct role in determining the attitudes and behavioural patterns, which in turn, affect the individual's perception and actions. It is methodologically, not feasible to arrive at appropriate generalizations without having a knowledge about the age, education, caste, religious and other background factors characterizing the respondents under study. Only after identifying such information on respondent's background, generalization can be drawn which can be related with other research studies. To understand the nature of the social grouping as well as the quality of interrelationship that exists among the members, it is essential to understand their demographic background. The demographic variables of the respondents included age, marital status, number of children, sex of the children. Young women are expected to behave differently as compared with elderly women. Marital status is also linked with differential perception towards sexual harassment. Additionally, the presence or absence of children in the family gives rise to different types of role responsibilities to the mothers and accordingly they handle the problems at workplace.

AGE

The present study focuses on the problem of "Sexual Harassment of Women at Workplace". For quantitative analysis only those women were included in the sample, who were working in the private sector. It was assumed that in private sector the legislative enforcement is less and job insecurity is more, therefore, chances of harassment are likely to be more. Age plays a significant role in determining the status of individual. It is necessary to ascertain the age groups of the respondents.

TABLE 2.1
Age of the Respondents

Age (In Years)	*Frequency*	*Percent*
Below 25	35	17.5
25-35	117	58.5
35-45	45	22.5
Above 45	3	1.5
Total	200	100.0

Mean age of the respondents is 31.19.

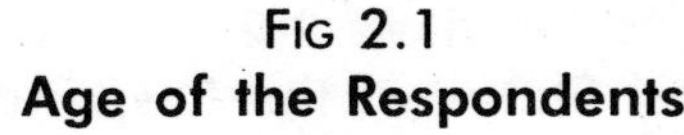

Fig 2.1
Age of the Respondents

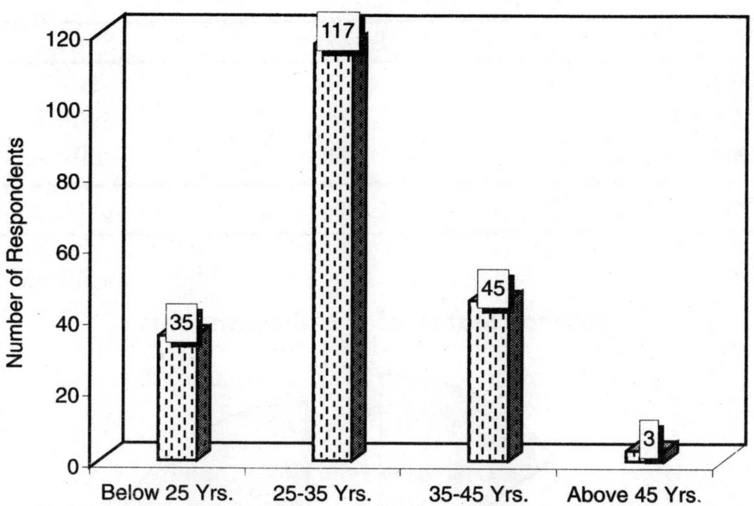

The data indicates that 58.5 percent of the total respondents were in the category of 25-35 years. 22.5 percent of the total respondents were in 35-45 years age group. In below 25 years age group there were 17.5 percent respondents. There were only 15.0 percent of the total respondents who belonged to above 45 years age group. The majority of the respondents were in the age groups of 25-45 years, which are the most productive years in a person's life.

MARITAL STATUS

In Indian society marriage is considered to be very important institution. In the present study an attempt has been made to study marital status of the working women. Some women start working when they are unmarried and many continue to work even after marriage. Dual earner couple is an emergent phenomenon. Similarly for widows, separated and divorced women economic necessity forces them to work outside home to make their living.

TABLE 2.2
Marital Status of the Respondents

Marital Status	*Frequency*	*Percent*
Never Married	76	38.0
Married	94	47.0
Once Married	30	15.0
Total	200	100.0

FIG. 2.2
Marital Status of the Respondents

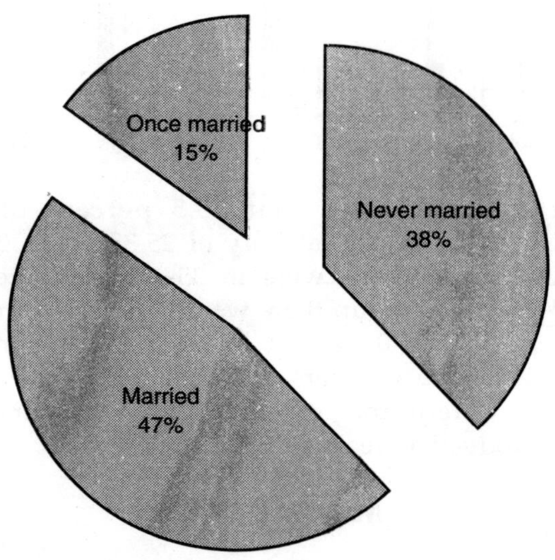

Results indicate that majority of the respondents in the study were married. Table 2.2 shows that 47.0 percent of the respondents were married and 38.0 percent respondents were never married. There were 15.0 percent of the respondents who were once married, but presently were single which included widows, divorced or separated women. Such results indicate that a large number of working women in the present study belonged to dual earner household. When a housewife takes the working role, she not only finds a change in her status within the family and outside it, but takes upon herself increasing pressure to reconcile the dual burden of two roles located in different sectors of the society; in house and workplace.

NUMBER OF CHILDREN

Presence or absence of children in the family is likely to affect the status of women in the society. Presence of more children in the family creates problem of management and economic burden on the family. An additional child will imply a decrease in time for mother to pursue her own interests. Each additional child increases the work load and conflicts. In our society, child care still remains under the domain of mothers and for any deviance on the part of the child it is the mother who is held responsible. An attempt has been made to find out the number of children of the respondents.

TABLE 2.3
Number of Children of Married Respondents

No. of children	*Frequency*	*Percent*
None	10	8.1
One-Two	34	64.5
Two-Four	84	27.4
Total	124	100.0

*76 respondents were unmarried.

Out of 124 respondents, majority of the respondents, i.e. 64.5 percent had up to two children and 27.4 percent of the respondents had up to four children. Such a distribution indicates that a large number of respondents in the present study had small family. They adhered to family planning. 8.1 percent of the respondents did not have any issue just because they were newly married or it included those respondents who got separated from their spouses immediately after marriage.

SEX OF THE CHILDREN

Presence of a male child is considered to be a status symbol in the Patriarchal society like India. Sex selective abortions in North-Western states of India highlight the fact that presence of male child in the family is considered must. The female child is not only considered liability but mothers who give birth to female child do not get much respect as compared to those who give birth to male child. Mothers of only girl children thus are expected to keep a low profile.

TABLE 2.4
Sex of the Children

No. of children	*Frequency*	*Percent*
Male	21	18.4
Female	13	11.4
Both	80	70.2
Total	114	100.0

*There were 114 respondents who had children.

Table 2.4 shows that 18.4 percent of the respondents had only male children, 11.4 percent had female children only, whereas, 70.2 percent of the respondents were blessed with both male and female children.

The Socio-economic variables considered for the present study included caste, religion, education, occupation, nature of the job and income of the respondents. An individual's social milieu not only influences his/her social position, network of relationships and contents of learning but also his social behaviour patterns. Social behaviour is a function of the life situations which may be physical, economical, social or psychological or interplay of these elements. It is assumed that persons having differential life situations would react differently to the same stimuli. It is, therefore, essential to explicate the role of these socio-economic variables.

CASTE

Caste system has a prominent place in the Indian social organization. It is a form of stratification in which an individual's position is fixed at birth. Traditionally, upper caste members always enjoyed a better access to the resources and services available in the society. There are some characteristics, which can be identified with one particular caste. For the purpose of study, the various castes of the respondents were divided into three main categories namely upper, intermediate and low castes.

TABLE 2.5
Caste of the Respondents

Caste	*Frequency*	*Percent*
Upper	113	56.5
Intermediate	49	24.5
Low	38	19.0
Total	200	100.0

FIG. 2 3
Caste of the Respondents

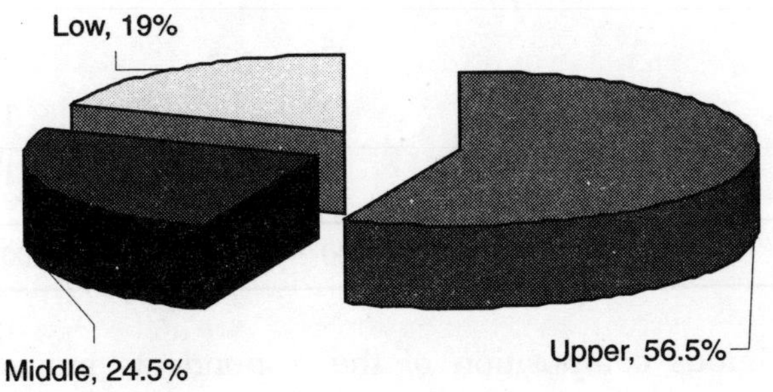

Data indicates that there were 56.5 percent respondents who belonged to the upper caste category while there were 24.5 percent in the intermediate caste category and only 19.0 percent respondents belonged to the low caste group. The results revealed that majority of the respondents belonged to the upper castes followed by the middle castes and quite a few respondents belonged to the low castes. The distribution of the respondents according to the caste background indicates a lower representation of backward and scheduled castes in the sample.

RELIGION

Religion is a belief in supernatural elements. Religion is that force which influences our ideology, value system and behaviour pattern. Most of the religions provide equality to women whereas religious preaching strict women's movement. Keeping such notion in mind religious background of the respondents was studied.

TABLE 2.6
Religion of the Respondents

Religion	*Frequency*	*Percent*
Hindu	150	75.0
Sikh	45	22.5
Muslim	2	1.0
Christian	3	1.5
Total	200	100.0

Religious composition of the respondents indicates that the majority of the respondents in present study belonged to Hindu religion. The percentage of Hindu population in the sample was 75.0 percent. The data shows that 22.5 percent were Sikh. Only 1.0 percent of the respondents were Muslims and 1.5 percent belonged to Christianity.

FIG. 2.4
Religion of the Respondents

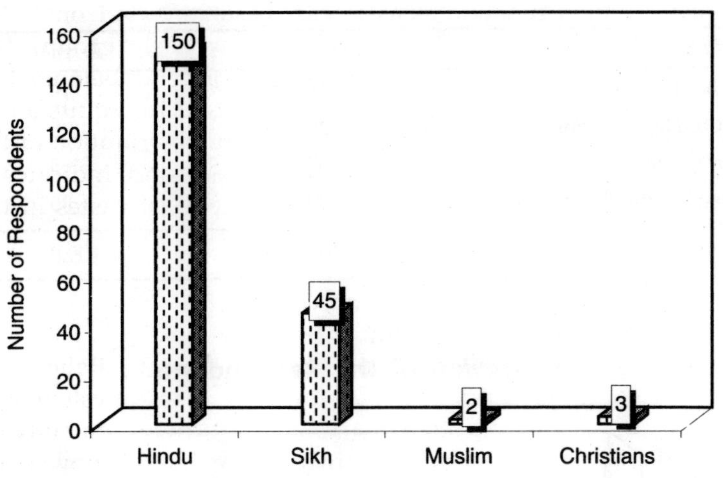

EDUCATION

Education is a channel through which human beings become more rational, develop the capacity to understand the reality. The educated women as compared to uneducated women are more aware of their rights; they can fight for their rights at workplace. Education helps in widening the perspective and exposes the individual to the world of opportunities and alternatives. Education is an important indicator of women's development. It is also an important instrument for attaining economic power and independence as it opens up opportunities that are linked with various levels of formal educational attainment.

The table indicates that 33.5 percent of the total respondents had educational qualification up to the level of Graduation and 35.0 percent had education upto the level of Post Graduation and above. Only 19.0 percent of the respondents were illiterate and 12.5 percent studied up to high school. Such findings indicate that large majority of working women in the present study were educated.

TABLE 2.7
Educational Qualification of the Respondents

Education	*Frequency*	*Percent*
Illiterate	38	19
Upto High School	25	12.5
Graduate	67	33.5
Post Graduate and above	70	35
Total	200	100.0

FIG. 2.5
Education of the Respondents

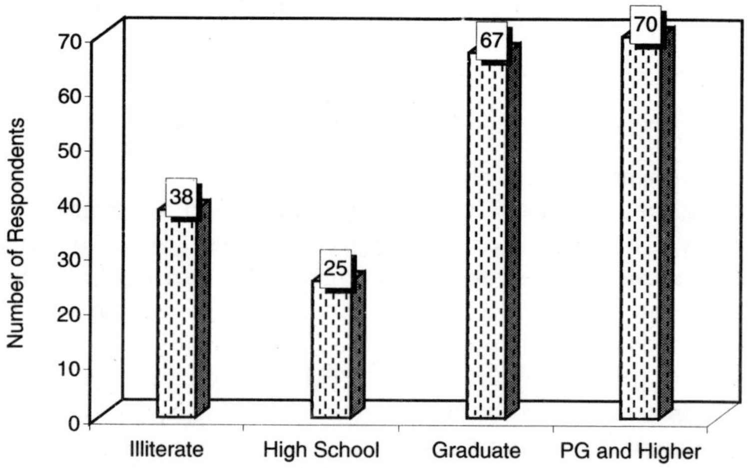

OCCUPATION OF RESPONDENTS

Occupation is a variable, which influences style of living as well as decision-making of an individual. Different occupations are associated with differential economic returns, prestige and authority. Sociologists have arranged different occupations in a hierarchical order. It was assumed that in private sector, legislative enforcement is less; therefore, chances of sexual harassment are likely to be more. For the present study, for the purpose of quantitative analysis, the women who work in private sector were included.

Women are taking up jobs due to various reasons. A few women work as sole supporters of the family while others work as additional bread-winners of the family. The occupation of the respondents has been graded into three categories, i.e. upper, middle and lower. Doctors, Administrative Officials and other Professionals have been included in upper category of occupations. The Administrative Staff, i.e. Receptionists, Clerks etc., women working in Call Centers, Stage Actresses, Nurses have been included in the middle category of occupations. Occupation in the lower category included Sweepers, Labourers, Construction Workers and Waitresses, etc.

TABLE 2.8
Occupation of the Respondents

Occupation	*Frequency*	*Percent*
Upper	66	33.0
Middle	93	46.5
Lower	41	20.5
Total	200	100.0

FIG. 2.6
Occupation of the Respondents

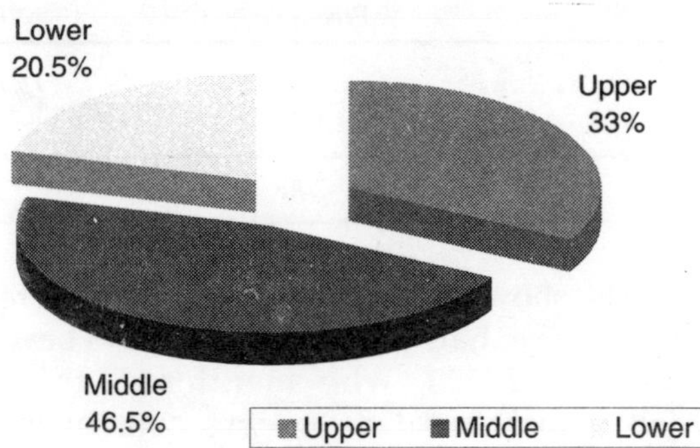

Findings highlight that majority of the respondents were in middle category of occupation, i.e. 46.5 percent followed by 33.0 percent in the upper category of occupation. 20.5 percent of the respondents were engaged in occupations of the lower category. For the present study, purposive sample of 200 women working in private sector has been taken. Different studies have indicated that majority of the working women get employment in middle level of occupations (Parthasarathy, 1990). Very few women are able to reach the top of the ladder due to many hurdles. Distribution of the data in the present study also highlights the fact majority of the women were concentrated in the middle level occupations.

NATURE OF JOB

For the purpose of quantitative analysis, the sample has been collected from the private sector. In the private sector no job is considered to be permanent. Yet, most of the respondents believed that their job is secure since they have been working for many years. Although liberalization of the market brought with it many job avenues, however, there is no permanency in the private sector. Many employees in the private sector shuttle between various jobs throughout their working career.

TABLE 2.9
Nature of Job

Nature of Job	*Frequency*	*Percent*
Temporary	80	40.0
Permanent	120	60.0
Total	200	100.0

The results show that 60.0 percent of the respondents reported that they had permanent job. There were 80 respondents out of 200, who mentioned that they had temporary job. It included daily wagers, construction workers, waitress, sweepers, actresses, women working as receptionists and in the call centers. It is clear from the above analysis that considerable number of women had been employed on temporary basis, majority were employed on permanent basis.

INCOME OF THE RESPONDENTS

Income determines the social status of individuals. Although income is an important variable for any study, yet it is a frivolous variable as it is difficult to know the exact income of a person. People have tendency to give wrong response when it comes to income. Therefore, in Social Sciences income cannot be treated as sole criterion for determination of social status. For the purpose of study and for analyzing the data, income of the respondents has been divided into three categories, i.e. low, middle and high income group. Low income group comprised of respondents whose income was below Rs. 5,000 per month. Medium income group included respondents having an income between Rs. 5,000–Rs. 20,000 per month and the high income group included respondents with income above Rs. 20,000 per month.

TABLE 2.10
Income of the Respondents

Income	*Frequency*	*Percent*
Low	41	20.5
Middle	91	45.5
High	68	34.0
Total	200	100.0

The data reveals that 45.5 percent of the respondents belonged to middle income group. 20.5 percent respondents belonged to low income group and 34.0 percent belonged to high-income group. Since majority of the respondents were engaged in middle level occupations, it is but natural that majority fall in the middle level category.

Fig. 2.7
Income of the Respondents

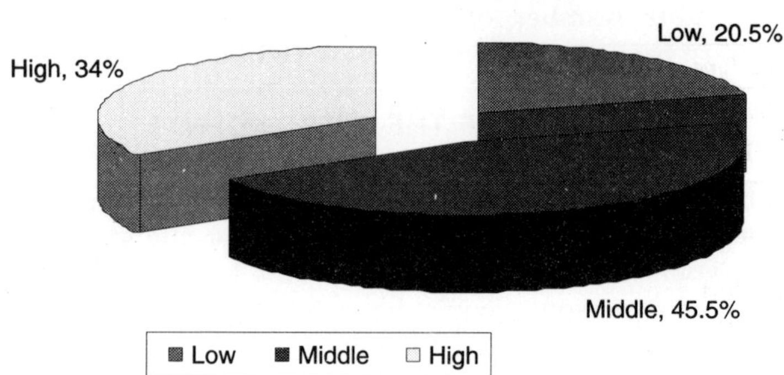

Family background of the respondents included their family composition, size of the family, education of the head of the family, economic status of the head of the family

FAMILY COMPOSITION

Family represents both an institution as well as an association. It is a group of individuals who are related to one another by blood ties, marriage or adoption and form an economic unit. It has remained the basic institution of Indian society where the dependency of younger members has remained for a longer duration. The female children continue to remain dependent on their parents till they are married and the male children till they become economically independent. Family members discharge mutual obligations for a considerable long time, which influences their style of life.

For the purpose of analysis, the family composition of respondents has been divided into two categories, i.e. Nuclear, Joint/Extended. Since the respondents belonged to different types of families. Some were living with their family of orientation while others with their family of procreation; it was decided to study family composition as it plays a crucial role in providing support to its members.

The data highlights that 73.0 percent of the respondents had nuclear families whereas 27.0 percent were living in joint/

TABLE 2.11
Family Types of the Respondents

Family Type	*Frequency*	*Percent*
Nuclear	146	73.0
Joint/Extended	54	27.0
Total	200	100.0

extended families. The household composition indicates that more than two-third of the respondents were residing in Nuclear households. As an outcome of the modernization of the society, the joint families are breaking up and in their places nuclear families are coming into existence. Chandigarh being a modern city with the physical structure, which does not encourage joint living yet it has been found approximately one-fourth of the respondents, were living in Joint/extended households. The data clearly reveals the dominance of nuclear family in the sample. The nuclear families maintain more open and healthy interaction between its members. It is assumed that respondents would also be discussing about their problems with family members.

SIZE OF THE FAMILY

The number of the family members is considered important with the assumption that the number of family members play a crucial role in providing support. The size of the family is crucial factor in highlighting interaction between its members. It was assumed that families with large size feel more confident. This gives strength to fight the atrocities of the outside world. For the present analysis, the size of the family included both family of orientation and family of procreation.

The data indicates that a majority of the respondents, i.e. 85.5 percent belonged to small size, i.e. members from two to four. It included respondents who were living with their parents only, children only, husband only, siblings only, husband and the child, mother and the child, parent and sibling, uncle and aunt, in-laws-husband-children, in-laws and

TABLE 2.12
Size of the Family

Size of family	*Frequency*	*Percent*
Alone	5	2.5
Small	171	85.5
Large	24	12.0
Total	200	100.0

husband, Grand parents-siblings, parents-siblings-uncle-aunt, siblings-uncle-aunt, only children. 12.0 percent of the respondents were in the category of more than 4. It included those respondents who were living with their parents and siblings, in-laws-husband-children, grand parents-parents-siblings, parents-in-laws-husband, parents-siblings-uncle-aunt, husband-children. 2.5 percent of the respondents were living alone. Very few respondents were staying alone. They were the only earning members of the family which showed that women were not depending on others for their livelihood. Most of them were staying either with their family of orientation or family of procreation. In such families too respondent's income was seen essential to run the family.

EDUCATIONAL QUALIFICATION OF THE HEAD OF FAMILY OF THE RESPONDENTS

Education in its wider sense includes everything that exerts a formative influence upon an individual. Educational qualification of the family members is of particular importance, since it is expected that educated family members can provide the respondents with better suggestions and solutions regarding their problems at work place.

The Table 2.13 shows that majority of the heads of the households in the present sample were Graduates and above. Since it included husbands and fathers of the respondents, a large number were highly qualified. In Indian society male literacy rate is higher than female literacy rate. There were 8.2 percent of the respondents whose head of family were

TABLE 2.13
Educational Qualification of the Head of the Family

Education	*Frequency*	*Percent*
Illiterate	53	27.2
Up to High School	16	8.2
Graduation and above	126	64.6
Total	195	100.0

* Since 5 respondents were staying alone, educational qualification of their family members was not procured.

educated up to High School, and 27.2 percent were illiterate. Since a sufficient number of respondent's family heads belonged to illiterate category, it is essential to discuss their profile. It has been found that illiterate family members were those who belonged to lower caste and class background. Further, many respondents had elderly parents and in-laws living with them who were illiterate.

ECONOMIC STATUS OF THE HEAD OF THE FAMILY OF THE RESPONDENTS

Along with educational qualification of the head of the family of the respondents occupational and economic statuses are also significant variables, which influence the respondent's life. It was assumed that an economically well-off family can contribute substantially for the welfare of its members. There is a positive correlation between the occupational status and economic status. The members with high occupational status occupy higher economic status.

For analyzing the economic status of the head of the family of the respondents, three categories were made, i.e. low, middle and high. Low income group comprised of those respondents where the head of the family had income below Rs. 5,000-Rs. 15,000 per month. Middle income group included income between Rs. 15,000-Rs. 30,000 per month. Upper income group included income of Rs. 30,000 and above per month.

TABLE 2.14
Income of the Head of the Family

Income (Per month)	*Frequency*	*Percent*
No Income	25	12.8
Low	43	22.0
Middle	37	18.9
High	90	46.3
Total	195	100.0

* Since 5 respondents were staying alone, occupational and economic status of their family members was not procured.

Table 2.14 shows that 46.3 percent of the respondents belonged to upper income group, followed by low income group, i.e. 22.0 percent. In 18.9 percent cases, head of family had income in the middle income group. There were however, 12.8 percent of respondents where the head of the family was not working, thus they had no income. These members were economically dependent upon the respondents. This category included those respondents who were once married, but presently staying with their parents, siblings or children. They were the only earning members in their family. It was assumed that economic necessity forces a person to tolerate inhumane and exploitative behaviour of the employee. Those respondents who are not the main breadwinner of the family can take the extreme step of leaving the job if harassment exists at the workplace.

To sum up the findings in this chapter, it was observed that:

- Maximum respondents belonged to the age group of 25-35 years.
- 47.0 percent of the respondents were married.
- Majority of the respondents had one-two children.
- Most of the respondents in the sample belonged to the Upper castes.
- Respondents in the sample were predominantly Hindus.

- Maximum respondents in the sample were educated.
- Majority of the respondents were engaged in occupation of middle level.
- Majority of respondents had permanent job.
- Majority of respondents belonged to medium income group.
- The predominant type of family was found to be nuclear family.
- Respondents by and large came from educated families.
- 46.1 percent respondent's families had an income above Rs. 30,000 per month belonging to upper income level and 12.8 percent of the respondent's family members were economically dependent on the respondents.

After explaining the background of the respondents, it becomes essential to understand the work environment of the respondents and their relationships with males at workplace. Since the present study focuses on sexual harassment of women at workplace, an attempt has been made in the next chapter to highlight the issues related to work place.

3

Work Environment

The world of work is changing, often drastically, due to the move towards a global economy characterized by greater openness or liberalization of markets, free or greater mobility of financial capital and people, and rapid distribution of products, information, technology, and consumption patterns. Typical of this process of globalization is the increased flexibility, casualization and informalization of employment and an expansion of atypical and precarious jobs. World-wide regular full-time wage employment has given way to a broad range of irregular forms of labour that are not covered by standard labour legislation, such as outsourcing, contract labour, home work, part-time work and self-employment in the informal sector. The rise of these jobs has been part of the business response to the changing market conditions and increased competition with a view to respond quickly to volatile demand and supply of capital. Labour costs are cut by reducing the number of 'core workers' and relying on irregular forms of employment in order to avoid labour surplus during economic downturns and paying for fringe benefits associated with decent work.

While providing new opportunities for economic growth, these changes have generated major challenges and rekindled concerns about the unfavourable global employment situation. Among the groups most affected are the young, the old and the less skilled, and, there is a 'bias against women in all these categories' (ILO, 2001).

Women are more likely to be working in 'men's jobs' than the opposite and this again increases chances of sexual harassment of women. As a rule, women are employed in a narrower range of occupations than men. In occupations where women are concentrated, such as teaching, they are usually in lower hierarchical positions. They dominate in clerical and secretarial jobs and in low-end occupations such as shop assistants, waitresses, maids, hair dressers, dress makers, teachers and nurses. Women are often seen in the lower categories of the job hierarchy. Discrimination exists not only in terms of wages, but also in terms of access to employment. Often women are found concentrated in occupations where the wage rates, as well as working conditions are poor and substandard. Low levels of skill on entry, lack of access to on-the-job training, employment histories punctuated by time spent, bearing and raising children, time off to care for family members and the assumption that men are the primary earners all contribute to the implicit assumption that women should be paid less then men.

Techno-social changes, which were accelerated in the Indian society, particularly after independence, not only provided opportunities for women to get modern education, but also opened up new avenues of gainful employment outside their homes. The rising cost of living, the perception of high standard of life, the new vocational training received in educational institutions and availability of jobs due to privatization of economy have created willingness on the part of women of middle and upper classes to seek gainful employment. The educated women of middle and upper classes started occupying white collar jobs whereas the uneducated rural women and women of weaker sections continued in the manual types of work. Such a situation not only brought the women into greater contacts with men at odd hours but also created barriers in their progress. These barriers come in the form of gender stereotypes regarding abilities, social attitudes about the proper place of women, in group exclusionary attitudes and practices on the part of women.

For appropriate performance of a role a particular setting is required, which is, congenial and helpful and facilitates the role incumbent to perform the role effectively and efficiently (Nadel, 1957). It was assumed that in addition to the personal attributes, the working conditions play a vital role in facilitating or jeopardizing role performance. As different types of organizations have different goals and procedures of work, we do expect that working conditions in private organizations would differ from Government and Semi-government organizations.

In India, in the last three decades, we have noticed a considerable increase in women at workplace in both organized and unorganized sector. The present section seeks to analyze the working environment of the respondents. It thus becomes essential to understand the working conditions under which women work before taking up their working relationship with their subordinates, colleagues and superordinates. It is necessary to know that the age at which the respondents started working, how did they get the job, what were the reasons of doing job, which features attracted them to opt for the job, what were the negative features of their job, what were their work hours, whether they worked in shift duties or traveled for work, etc. Further, an attempt has been made to know whether respondents faced any problem while being trained by male instructor. Many researchers have reported that women who work at odd hours, work in highly sexualized environment or travel for work are likely to face more problems than those who do not (Gruber, 1998; Gutek *et. al.*, 1990; Loe, 1996). Therefore, an effort has been made to get information on these matters. Without knowing answers to all these questions, the study would remain incomplete.

SECTION I

AGE AT THE TIME OF STARTING WORK

The present study focuses on the problem of "Sexual Harassment of Women at Workplace", however, women who were working in private sector were included in the sample. It was assumed that in private sector, the legislative enforcement is less and job insecurity is more, therefore chances for harassment are likely to be more. It is important to know at what age the respondents started working. When women start working at an early age, it is mainly due to economic necessity. Researchers have indicated that economic necessity results in exploitation at workplace. Park (2007) revealed that women aged 19 to 40 years old were forced to have sex under threat of being sacked.

TABLE 3.1
Age at the Time of Starting Work

Age (in years)	*Frequency*	*Percent*
Below 20 Years	31	15.5
20-25 Years	103	51.5
25-35 Years	66	33.0
Total	200	100.0

For the purpose of analysis, the age at which respondents started working was divided into three categories. The data indicates that 51.5 percent of the total respondents started working in the age group of 20-25 years. 33.0 percent of the respondents started working in the age group of 25-35 years. There were 15.5 percent of the respondents who started working at younger age, i.e. below the age of 20 years mainly due to economic necessity. These respondents were engaged in unskilled occupations which did not require any specialized training or education. These respondents fall in the category of the vulnerable group. Thus, it was found in the present study, maximum percentage of the respondents started working in the age group of 20-25 years, as these are the most productive years in a person's life. Such findings also indicated that these respondents started working when they were of marriageable age.

MODE OF RECRUITMENT

For the present study, it is necessary to know that how the respondents got their jobs. In the government sector the recruitment is done through employment exchange. For some posts written tests followed by interviews are conducted for the candidates to get their entry. In private sectors jobs are mostly advertised; personal influences, contacts also play an important role in the mode of recruitment.

TABLE 3.2
Mode of Recruitment

Mode of Recruitment	*Frequency*	*Percent*
Formal	113	56.5
Informal	87	43.5
Total	200	100.0

Table 3.2 indicates that 56.5 percent of the respondents got job through formal contact, i.e. newspaper and advertisement. 43.5 percent of the respondents got their job with help of others. It was through personal contacts, through primary relative or through known person, women got jobs in unorganized sector. Influence, as a source of recruitment was found mostly in unskilled jobs. There is not much difference in informal and formal mode of recruitment. The data revealed that majority of the respondents got job with own efforts.

REASONS FOR WORKING

As time is changing, the notion for women going out to work is also changing. The results have indicated that a large number of working women in the present study belonged to dual earner household. Women have started working outside their homes for various reasons. In the present study, it is very important to know that why women have started working outside the home. What are the reasons, which forced women to go out of their homes? Rani (1976) cited three reasons that motivated women to seek jobs outside their traditional roles: economic monetary gain, social role enhancement and personal reasons. Women of middle class are compelled, in the changed economic conditions, to enter into jobs to earn their livelihood. Also, a large number of married women take up work as their husband's incomes are no longer adequate to meet the needs of the family. Apart from economic necessities, there are other reasons for employment of women. These reasons relate to the desire for economic independence, utilization of individual talent, trying to secure equality of status and utilizing time and energy in order to reduce monotony and boredom from domestic life.

TABLE 3.3
Reasons for Working

Reasons	*Frequency*	*Percent*
Necessity	83	41.5
Economic independence	40	20.0
Personal development	24	12.0
Miscellaneous	53	26.5
Total	200	100.0

For the purpose of analysis, the reasons of undertaking a job were divided into four categories. The data revealed that 41.5 percent of the respondents started working because of the economic necessity. The necessity referred to no source of income, loss of the breadwinner or the meager economic resources to support the family. 26.5 percent of the respondents started working for fun sake, time pass. They were not interested in any career but got job. These cases had accepted the job, as they had no specific preferences in their mind. 20.0

percent of the respondents started working to get the economic independence. They wanted to be economically independent irrespective of the job contents for the attributes of their occupational role. 12.0 percent of the respondents started working for their own personal development. As they were interested in a career and got job, in these cases it was the personal growth which was important. The data revealed that majority of the respondents started working outside the homes because of their economic needs. A few respondents started working for other reasons such as economic independence, personal development, etc. Hemlatha and Suryanarayana (1983) in their study reported that 62.0 percent were working for economic reasons, i.e. to support the family, to supplement the family income and to contribute to raising family standards of living. Parikh and Garg (1987) mentioned that the economic dimension is very significant. Many Women had taken up jobs for economic security.

ATTRACTIVE FEATURES OF THE JOB

The above discussion supports contention that in the beginning only those women opted for jobs that were forced by special circumstances but now a large number of women are opting for jobs as choice. Economic security may attract some women to jobs. There are others who give importance to position, freedom and personal development.

TABLE 3.4
Attractive Features of the Job

Attractive Features	*Frequency*	*Percent*
Money	83	41.5
Good work atmosphere	61	30.5
Less working hours	14	7.0
Work place in close proximity	9	4.5
No reply	33	16.5
Total	200	100.0

With globalization and liberalization of economy in India, private sector is increasing swiftly in comparison to government sector. These days, private sector is giving good salary to employees as compared to government sector, i.e. why people are approaching private sector in large number. Data in table 3.4 indicates that there were 41.5 percent of the respondents who were working because it fulfilled their financial requirements. They just stepped into the job, which they came across. They were working mainly due to monetary reasons. For them economic gains associated with job was the main attraction. There were 30.5 percent of the respondents that reported good atmosphere at work place as main attraction of their job. Women coming from lower or lower middle class family found atmosphere at their workplace good. They were sitting in an air-conditioned office with educated people that provided them status. There were 7.0 percent of the respondents, who gave importance to less working hours; these women mainly belonged to Dual-Earner households. They found their regular work hours very comfortable because this way they were able to make a balance between their family and work place. This condition was applicable in 4.5 percent of the cases who reported that their workplace was in close proximity to their residence. They did not have to travel long distance and were able to take care of their home and workplace. Findings endorse the views of Inminia (1965) who reported that the majority of married women found their jobs pleasant and were satisfied with the financial returns of their jobs.

FORMAL TRAINING

When a woman opts for an occupational role, it is expected that she would acquaint herself with the nature of work she is expected to perform. This knowledge may be acquired prior to one's entry into an occupational role or at the time of acceptance of job. The finer details and the implications may be learned through in service training. However, prior knowledge not only help the new recruit to calculate the benefits but also helps her in subsequent training and acceptance of the norms governing her occupational role.

It was in this context that information was sought from respondents whether they had acquired any training or not.

The following table also shows that how many of the respondents got formal training after joining the job.

TABLE 3.5
Formal Training of the Respondents

Formal training	*Frequency*	*Percent*
Yes	44	22.0
No	156	78.0
Total	200	100.0

Table 3.5 shows that a large number, i.e. 78.0 percent of the respondents did not get any formal training after joining the job. Only 22.0 percent of the respondents got formal training. Since the women in present study were engaged in wide variety of occupations as such they were not given any formal training. Women who were engaged in technical jobs were given formal training. Results indicate that a majority of respondents did not have any formal training.

IF YES, SEX OF THE TRAINERS

After obtaining information on number of women respondents who got formal training, it was decided to procure information about the trainers who trained them.

TABLE 3.5.1
Sex of the Trainers

Sex	*Frequency*	*Percent*
Male	15	34.1
Female	4	9.1
Both	25	56.8
Total	44	100.0

* 78.0 percent were such respondents who did not get any formal training.

Results show that 56.8 percent of the respondents were trained by both male and female instructors. 34.1 percent were trained by male instructors only and 9.1 percent were trained by female instructors only.

HARASSMENT BY MALE INSTRUCTORS

For the present study, it is important to know whether respondents experienced any harassment by male instructors or not. Fiske and Neuberg (1990) reported that men have little history or experience of dealing with women in the job react on the basis of limited information, thereby promoting stereotypes and heightening the probability of sexual harassment. Mahajan (1982) in a study of Indian Police Women highlighted the difficulties faced by police women when trained by male instructors.

TABLE 3.5.1.1
Respondents who Faced Harassment by Male Instructors

Harassment by male instructors	*Frequency*	*Percent*
Yes	6	15.0
No	34	85.0
Total	40	100.0

* 78.0 percent of the respondents did not get any formal training and 2.0 percent of the respondents were trained by female instructors.

Table 3.5.1.1 shows that 85.0 percent of the respondents did not face any harassment by the male instructors. The respondents found the atmosphere at the training was quite congenial. Only 6 respondents reported that they faced harassment while being trained by the male instructors. Harassed respondents experienced sexual remarks and touching by the male instructors. The harassed respondents reported that they were made to stay late purposely.

NUMBER OF WORK HOURS

A number of studies have reported that women who work late hours face more harassment. Hemlatha and Suryanarayana (1983) found that women working at odd hours faced more problems than those working at regular hours. For the present study, it is important to know working hours of the respondents. It was assumed that women who work late hours are likely to get more harassed as compared to women who work in normal working hours.

TABLE 3.6
Work-hours of the Respondents

Work Hours	*Frequency*	*Percent*
> 8 hours	126	63.0
8 - 12 hours	74	37.0
Total	200	100.0

Table 3.6 indicates that on the whole 63.0 percent of the respondents worked for 8 hours, i.e. normal work hours and 37.0 percent worked for 8-12 hours. In the present study, Doctors, Nurses, Journalists, Actresses were working for 8-12 hours. The data revealed that maximum of the respondents work for normal hours. Pradhan-Malla (2001) reported that women working in hospitals are more likely to be sexually harassed because they work late and in shift duties.

SHIFT DUTY

An attempt has been made to find the nature of job of working women in the present study. It was reported that the chances of sexual harassment are more in the private sector due to less legislative enforcement. Although people are paid quite handsomely they have to work late and even at night. The problem is particularly acute for workers who work late during the evening or at night on overtime, second or third shifts. Women coming home from work late at night are particularly fearful since, in addition to the 'normal' quota of harassment, they can also be picked up by the police on suspicion of prostitution. Men frequently make abusive catcalls; lewd and obscene comments to the women workers, sometimes following them to make threatening sexual advances. According to a woman leader of a trade union, when the men in the factory cannot harass the women in the factory, they harass them outside the factory (Huda, 2001). Hospitals, hotels, call centers recruit women employees, due to the requirement of the job. Women have to work in shift duties. These women are more likely to face the problem of sexual harassment. Keeping this in mind respondents were asked to state whether they worked in shift duties.

TABLE 3.7
Respondents Working in Shift Duties

Shift Duty	*Frequency*	*Percent*
Yes	47	23.5
No	153	76.5
Total	200	100.0

The table indicates that 23.5 percent of the respondents worked in shift duties and 76.5 percent of the respondents did not work in shift duties. Those respondents who were engaged in shift duty included, Doctors, Nurses, Receptionists, Journalists, Actresses and Sweepers.

FREQUENCY OF SHIFT DUTY

As the above table shows that 23.5 percent of the respondents worked in shift duties, it is also important to know how frequently these women were doing shift duties. Since majority of women engaged in shift duties were working in Hospitals, Hotels and Call Centers, it was assumed most of the respondents would be frequently working in shift duties.

TABLE 3.7.1
Frequency of Shift Duty

Shift Duty	*Frequency*	*Percent*
Rarely	12	25.5
Frequently	35	74.5
Total	47	100.0

* 76.5 percent of the respondents did not work in shift duties.

The data indicates that 74.5 percent of the respondents frequently worked in shift duties. 25.5 percent of the respondents rarely worked in shift duty. Women engaged in Journalism and Theatre rarely worked in shift duties. Such results indicated that women work in shift duties as per the requirements of their jobs.

TRAVELLING

There are various problems faced by working women who travel for their work assignments. Even by virtue of being working women and earning members of the family, they do not have the privilege to move freely, to demand equal treatment and the like. They may have to travel for a night or more with their male colleagues, bosses or juniors. A man can go to a new place, stay in a hotel and attend to his work without an escort, but a woman had to be more careful about her stay. To that extent women are more vulnerable to exploitation. Many workers also faced sexual harassment

TABLE 3.8
Respondents who Travelled for Work Assignments

Travelling	*Frequency*	*Percent*
Yes	37	18.5
No	163	81.5
Total	200	100.0

problems on their way to and from work, especially where there was lack of access to safe transportation facilities. Even the bus drivers and helpers on the bus treated them condescendingly and harassed sexually (Huda, 2001).

Table 3.8 indicates that 81.5 percent of the respondents did not travel regarding the work assignments and 18.5 percent of the respondents travelled for their work assignment. After a long conversation, it was also found that male officials always accompanied them. The women who travelled for their work assignments were Administrative Officers, Journalists and Nurses. Majority of these women were in the age group of 25-35 years. Now, it is also important to know that how often these women travel.

TABLE 3.8.1
Frequency of Travel

Frequency of travel	*Frequency*	*Percent*
Rarely	26	70.3
Frequent	5	13.5
Sometimes	6	16.2
Total	37	100.0

* 81.5 percent of the respondents did not travel for work.

An attempt has been made to find out the frequency of travelling. Women who travelled frequently for work faced number of problems. Women have not only right to work but also to work under right conditions. The data indicates that 70.3 percent of the women travelled rarely. 16.2 percent of the women travelled sometimes and 13.5 percent women travelled frequently for the work assignments. Such results indicated that even if women were travelling for work in the present study their number and frequency of travel was very less.

To sum up the findings in this section, it was observed that:

- Maximum respondents started working in the age group of 20-25 years.

- Majority of the respondents got their jobs through formal source.
- Majority of the respondents worked because of economic need.
- The respondents who were trained by male instructors experienced sexual harassment during training.
- Maximum respondents had normal working hours.
- Doctors, Nurses, Journalists, Receptionists, Actresses and Waitresses worked in shift duties.
- 18.5 percent of the total respondents travelled for work assignments, out of which 2.5 percent travelled frequently.

SECTION II

RELATIONSHIPS WITH MALES AT WORKPLACE

According to Goffman (1961), the nature of interactions is influenced by social definitions, values and norms. How an individual should behave towards the subordinates, colleagues and superordinates is determined by the conventions and formal definitions of the organization in which she is working. It is perhaps in this context that Hinde (1979) reminds us that relationships can never be fully understood in isolation from the social context. The type of relationships the individual has with their subordinates will be completely different from that with their colleagues and superiors. The type of group relationships, which emerge and develop between the female colleagues, may not have the same content and quality of relationships when the colleague group is heterosexual. Social definitions may debar the women to develop close personal relationships with the superiors, which may be the desired thing for the males.

An attempt has been made in the second section of this present chapter to find out the relationships that working women have with their colleagues, superordinates and subordinates at workplace.

RELATIONS WITH COLLEAGUES

The members of a colleague group have almost the same status. They interact with each other as equals. They cooperate for their own as well as for the goals of the organization in which they work. As the members of a colleague group are almost equal to each other, they are expected to plan their actions together and for the attainment of goals they are required to co-ordinate their activities.

Maintaining relations with male colleagues is another big problem. Those of equal status may be jealous of women if they are successful as they threaten their position. Theoretically, a woman worker in a workplace is equal to any male worker in identical position with regard to powers and privileges as well as performance and prerogatives. However, in actual practice, this may be blurred by the prevailing notions about women. If society considers women as inferior to men, her position in the workplace will be influenced by this prejudice no matter what her legal rights and actual capabilities are. In other words, her claim to equality greatly depends upon how the colleagues at the workplace treat her.

RELATIONS WITH SUPERORDINATES

The nature of human interactions is influenced by social definitions as well as by the positions the interacting persons occupy. The women employees' relationship with male superordinates is very important. Miller (1998) has labeled the top authority individuals as a 'highly-conscious' group. The top authority individuals are not only self-conscious but conscious of their 'self-importance'. Their ethnocentrism leads them to believe that they have special gifts and attributes not generally shared by the commoners. It is perhaps for this reason that they keep a distance from their subordinates. Men at the top of the supervisory structure are vested with the right of decision-making and commanding. It is therefore, but natural that they develop a bossy personality configuration. It is the duty of women employees to receive orders from their superordinates and execute them as per rules. The treatment they get from their superiors is an indicator of the pattern of discrimination or otherwise, shown to them. Getting due respect or treatment may be considered as an indicator of men's recognition of their capacity for equal work.

RELATIONS WITH SUBORDINATES

An individual is expected to play his/her role keeping in view the position he/she is holding in society. However, the expectations differ from one cultural context to another. During working hours the high authority individuals are expected to keep a permissible distance from their subordinates. However, there is a general apprehension that if the superordinates become friendly with the subordinates they would neither be able to get the work done from their subordinates nor could they exercise authority over them. It is, therefore, demanded that the superordinates should maintain a reasonable distance from their subordinates. When the women are in the position of superordinate, how readily her orders are accepted and appreciated by male subordinates is a question that needs addressal. Subordinates may not be readily disposed to accept the authority of women in superior positions. In that case women do not get a fair deal from their subordinates.

Before understanding the relationships of women with the males at workplace, it is important to know the number of colleagues, superordinates and subordinates, the working women have. Table 3.9 presents the distribution of number of colleagues, superordinates and subordinates at work place

It was observed that 64.0 percent, 56.0 percent and 64.2 percent of the respondents had more than 5 colleagues, superordinates and subordinates, respectively. It showed that majority of the women were engaged in prestigious occupations. All the respondents had male colleagues and superordinates. But there were seven respondents who did not have any male subordinates, since these respondents were engaged in lower occupations. The subordinates of other respondents of lower occupations were taken on the basis, who were earning low income than the respondents.

Further, an attempt was made to understand the relationships of women with their male colleagues,

TABLE 3.9
Number of Colleagues, Superordinates and Subordinates at Workplace

Number of males	*Colleagues*	*Superordinates*	*Subordinates*
1-2	38 19%	51 25.5%	32 16.6%
2-5	34 17%	37 18.5%	37 19.2%
5+	128 64%	112 56%	124 64.2%
Total	200	200	193

* 7 represents did not have subordinates.

superordinates and subordinates in relation to their age, caste, religion, marital status and occupation.

AGE AND RELATIONSHIP WITH MALE COLLEAGUES, SUPERORDINATES AND SUBORDINATES

An attempt was made to find out relationship between age and relation with male colleagues, superordinates and subordinates. Age is an important indicator, which affects relationships of individual with their colleagues, superordinates and subordinates. It was assumed that respondents belonging to different age group would have different relations with their male colleagues, superordinates and subordinates. Devi (1982) found that those women who were of younger age but occupied higher occupational position enjoyed higher respect from their subordinates.

Table 3.10 shows that maximum uncordial relations with male colleagues, superordinates and subordinates were among the respondents in the age group of 25-35 years, i.e. 88.2 percent with colleagues, 75.2 percent with superordinates and 76.7 percent with subordinates. It has been found that women of younger age group in the present study were involved in occupations of low prestige. These women were economically needy and unaware of their rights at workplace. They worked

TABLE 3.10
Age of the Respondents and Relationship with Male Colleagues, Superordinates and Subordinates

Age (in Yrs.)	*Colleagues*			*Superordinates*			*Subordinates*		
	Cordial	*Normal*	*Un-cordial*	*Cordial*	*Normal*	*Un-cordial*	*Cordial*	*Normal*	*Un-cordial*
(1)	*(2)*	*(3)*	*(4)*	*(5)*	*(6)*	*(7)*	*(8)*	*(9)*	*(10)*
Below 25	10 28.6%	22 34.9%	3 2.9%	7 24.1%	15 39.5%	13 9.8%	8 30.7%	15 31.9%	10 8.3%
25-35	18 51.4%	9 14.3%	90 88.2%	9 31.1%	8 21.0%	100 75.2%	15 57.7%	10 21.3%	92 76.7%
Above 35	7 20.0%	32 50.8%	9 8.9%	13 44.8%	15 39.5%	20 15.0%	3 11.6%	22 46.8%	18 15.0%
Total	35	63	102	29	38	133	26	47	120

* For colleagues N is 200, for superordinates N is 200, for subordinates N is 193, since 7 respondents did not have subordinates.

for economic necessity, were not in position to lose their job. The age group of 25-35 years is the most productive years in any individual's life. Majority of the respondents in this age group were placed in good occupational positions. These women did not feel inferior to men in any respect. Majority of women in this age group were married, mothers of children, educated, engaged in occupations of middle level and had complete awareness of their rights. They did not hesitate to report any unpleasant experience they developed at work place with their male colleagues, superordinates and subordinates. Findings indicated that women in age group of 25-35 years had more uncordial relations with their male colleagues, superordinates and subordinates. Findings coincide with results of Devi (1982).

MARITAL STATUS AND RELATIONS WITH MALE COLLEAGUES, SUPERORDINATES AND SUBORDINATES

Table 3.11 presents the relationship between marital status and relation with male colleagues, superordinates and subordinates. It was assumed that women who had triple burden of home, occupation and children are likely to have adjustment problems with males at workplace. The working women have to suffer a number of psychological problems created by the male co-workers and the male boss. Moreover, if she happens to be unmarried/widow/divorcee the problem will be much more complicated. Because, the male boss with the advantage of his position and official status may try to exploit her (Devi, 1982).

Results indicated that majority of the respondents who were married had uncordial relations with male colleagues, superordinates and subordinates, i.e. 63.7 percent with colleagues, 52.6 percent with superordinates and 62.5 percent with subordinates. These results contradict the findings of Devi (1982) who reported that unmarried/widow/divorcee women are more vulnerable to harassment because of their marital status.

Table 3.11

Marital Status of the Respondents and Relationship with Male Colleagues, Superordinates and Subordinates

Marital Status	Colleagues			Superordinates			Subordinates		
	Cordial	*Normal*	*Un-cordial*	*Cordial*	*Normal*	*Un-cordial*	*Cordial*	*Normal*	*Un-cordial*
(1)	(2)	(3)	(4)	(5)	(6)	(7)	(8)	(9)	(10)
Presently Single	23 65.7%	46 73.1%	37 36.3%	13 44.8%	30 78.9%	63 47.4%	16 61.5%	40 85.1%	45 37.5%
Married	12 34.3%	17 26.9%	65 63.7%	16 55.2%	8 21.1%	70 52.6%	10 38.5%	7 14.9%	75 62.5%
Total	35	63	102	29	38	133	26	47	120

* The category single at present, included those respondents who were unmarried, widowed, separated

**For colleagues N is 200, for superordinates N is 200 and for subordinates N is 193.

CASTE AND RELATIONSHIP WITH MALE COLLEAGUES, SUPERORDINATES AND SUBORDINATES

Caste is an important characteristic in Indian context. Table 3.4 describes the relationship between caste and relationship with colleagues, superordinates and subordinates. In order to know the profile of women who had uncordial relations with colleagues, superordinates and subordinates, it was decided to know the caste background. Different research studies have indicated that people like to interact with individuals of their own caste groups. They hesitate to interact freely with members of lower or upper caste, many times individuals are harassed because of their caste background.

Findings indicate that majority of the respondents who had uncordial relations with colleagues, superordinates and subordinates belonged upper caste group, i.e. 78.4 percent with the colleagues, 73.7 percent with the superordinates and 85.0 percent with the subordinates. On the other hand women belonging to lower and intermediate castes had cordial and normal relations with colleagues, superordinates and subordinates. Such findings indicated that women of upper caste faced more problems with the male colleagues, superordinates and subordinates as compared to middle and lower caste group, because they were more sensitive in maintaining relations with males at the workplace.

RELIGION AND RELATIONSHIP WITH MALE COLLEAGUES, SUPERORDINATES AND SUBORDINATES

An individual's outlook towards herself, her fellow beings is coloured by the religious doctrine she has received. Thus, religious background differentiates between individuals. Individuals develop close bond with persons of their own religion. Table 3.13 presents the relationship between religion and relation with colleagues, superordinates and subordinates. An attempt has been made to find out that whether women interact with colleagues, superordinates and subordinates on the basis of religion.

The religious distribution of the sample indicated that majority of Hindus had uncordial relations with colleagues,

TABLE 3.12

Caste of the Respondents and Relationship with Male Colleagues, Superordinates and Subordinates

Caste	*Colleagues*			*Superordinates*			*Subordinates*		
	Cordial	*Normal*	*Un-cordial*	*Cordial*	*Normal*	*Un-cordial*	*Cordial*	*Normal*	*Un-cordial*
(1)	*(2)*	*(3)*	*(4)*	*(5)*	*(6)*	*(7)*	*(8)*	*(9)*	*(10)*
Upper	9 25.7%	24 38.1%	80 78.4%	10 34.5%	5 13.2%	98 73.7%	4 15.4%	7 14.9%	102 85.0%
Inter-mediate	15 42.9%	14 22.2%	20 19.6%	9 31.0%	10 26.3%	30 22.6%	12 46.1%	21 44.7%	16 13.3%
Lower	11 31.4%	25 39.7%	2 2.0%	10 34.5%	23 60.5%	5 3.7%	10 38.5%	19 40.4%	2 17.0%
Total	35	63	102	29	38	133	26	47	120

* For colleagues N is 200, for superordinates N is 200, for subordinates N is 193, since 7 respondents did not have subordinates.

TABLE 3.13

Religion of the Respondents and Relationship with Male Colleagues, Superordinates and Subordinates

Religion	*Colleagues*			*Superordinates*			*Subordinates*		
	Cordial	*Normal*	*Un-cordial*	*Cordial*	*Normal*	*Un-cordial*	*Cordial*	*Normal*	*Un-cordial*
(1)	*(2)*	*(3)*	*(4)*	*(5)*	*(6)*	*(7)*	*(8)*	*(9)*	*(10)*
Hindu	22 62.8%	30 47.6%	98 96.1%	16 55.2%	23 60.5%	111 83.5%	6 23.1%	39 82.9%	98 81.6%
Sikh	9 25.8%	33 52.4%	3 2.9%	9 31.2%	15 39.5%	21 15.7%	16 61.5%	8 17.1%	21 17.5%
Muslim	2 5.7%	0 0.0%	0 0.0%	2 6.8%	0 0.0%	0 0.0%	2 7.7%	0 0.0%	0 0.0%
Christian	2 5.7%	0 0.0%	1 1.0%	2 6.8%	0 0.0%	1 0.8%	2 7.7%	0 0.0%	0 0.0%
Total	35	63	102	29	38	133	26	47	120

* For colleagues N is 200, for superordinates N is 200, for subordinates N is 193, since 7 respondents did not have subordinates.

superordinates and subordinates, i.e. 96.1 percent, 83.5 percent and 81.6 percent respectively. Such distinction was not found in other religious groups. In the present study majority of respondents belonged to Hindu religion, such findings show that relationships at workplace are not measured on the basis of religion.

EDUCATION AND RELATIONSHIP WITH MALE COLLEAGUES, SUPERORDINATES AND SUBORDINATES

In order to find out the possible influence of education on relations with male colleagues, superordinates and subordinates, education has been analyzed with relationships. Educational level determines the occupation of the respondent. Women with higher educational qualification are engaged in occupations of higher prestige. Very few women however make to higher occupational positions as majority of them are not well qualified. Sivaprakasan & Suriakala (2003) argued that the male superior's attitude vary with the educational qualifications possessed by their female employees. Those who are highly qualified are well respected by male superiors than those who possessed less qualification.

Results show that more educated respondents had uncordial relations with male colleagues, superordinates and subordinates, i.e. 87.3 percent with male colleagues, 91.0 percent with superordinates and 85.0 percent with subordinates. Among the educated respondents, 12.5 percent were educated up to high school, 33.5 percent were Graduate and 35.0 percent were Postgraduate and above. It was assumed that since educated respondents were more aware about their rights at the workplace, they would not hesitate to report uncordial relations with males at workplace. Whereas uneducated women were unaware of their rights, were economically needy and required job to fulfil their basic requirements; they would hesitate to report uncordial relations at workplace. Findings do not endorse the results of Sivaprakasan & Suriakala (2003).

TABLE 3.14

Education of the Respondents and Relationship with Male Colleagues, Superordinates and Subordinates

Education	*Colleagues*			*Superordinates*			*Subordinates*		
	Cordial	*Normal*	*Un-cordial*	*Cordial*	*Normal*	*Un-cordial*	*Cordial*	*Normal*	*Un-cordial*
(1)	*(2)*	*(3)*	*(4)*	*(5)*	*(6)*	*(7)*	*(8)*	*(9)*	*(10)*
Illiterate	10 28.6%	15 23.8%	13 12.7%	15 51.7%	11 28.9%	12 9.0%	4 15.4%	9 19.1%	18 15.0%
Educated	25 71.4%	48 76.2%	89 87.3%	14 48.3%	27 71.1%	121 91.0%	22 84.6%	38 80.9%	102 85.0%
Total	35	63	102	29	38	133	26	47	120

* For colleagues N is 200, for superordinates N is 200, for subordinates N is 193, since 7 respondents did not have subordinates.

OCCUPATION AND RELATIONS WITH MALE COLLEAGUES, SUPERORDINATES AND SUBORDINATES

The association between occupation of the respondents and relation with male colleagues, superordinates and subordinates is essential to study the work relations.Since the present study pertains to sexual harassment at workplace, it has been reported that women who work in male dominated occupations and non-traditional jobs are more vulnerable to harassment (European Commission, 1999). Devi (1982) reported that women with high occupational levels received greater respect from male colleagues as compared to women engaged in occupations of lower prestige.

Majority of the respondents who had uncordial relations with male colleagues, superordinates and subordinates were engaged in occupations of middle category, followed by respondents who were engaged in occupations of upper category respondents. There was not much difference in the percentages. Women engaged in occupations of middle and upper level were educated, had awareness of their rights and were confident enough to report uncordial relations with males at workplace. It is important to keep in mind that women through the centuries in many parts of the world, have been perceived to be, and therefore are socially conditioned from an early age to be subordinate to men. Inequalities in the position of men and women exist in nearly all societies. Women are expected to be sexually passive and men are socialized to be sexually aggressive. Women become targets of dishonour when they are seen to be competing for power or take on new roles. In many societies and situations men are more likely to harass the women as they are often placed in more senior or better-paid positions. Results show that women engaged in lowly paid occupation, hesitated to report uncordial relations at workplace. Further, these women were working because of economic necessity and they were not interested in any controversy. Findings do not coincide with results of Devi (1982).

Findings reported that women of lower caste and occupation of lower prestige had comfortable relations with men at workplace. These illiterate women lacked awareness of

TABLE 3.15

Occupation of the Respondents and Relationship with Male Colleagues, Superordinates and Subordinates

Occupation	*Colleagues*			*Superordinates*			*Subordinates*		
	Cordial	*Normal*	*Un-cordial*	*Cordial*	*Normal*	*Un-cordial*	*Cordial*	*Normal*	*Un-cordial*
(1)	*(2)*	*(3)*	*(4)*	*(5)*	*(6)*	*(7)*	*(8)*	*(9)*	*(10)*
Upper	6 17.1%	14 22.2%	46 45.1%	3 10.4%	8 21.1%	55 41.4%	4 15.4%	8 17.0%	54 45.0%
Middle	14 40.0%	30 47.6%	49 48.0%	13 44.8%	20 52.6%	60 45.1%	14 53.8%	20 42.6%	59 49.2%
Lower	15 42.9%	19 30.2%	7 6.9%	13 44.8%	10 26.3%	18 13.5%	8 30.8%	19 40.4%	7 5.8%
Total	35	63	102	29	38	133	26	47	120

* For colleagues N are 200, for superordinates N is 200, for subordinates N is 193, since 7 respondents did not have subordinates.

their rights. Further, they could not afford to loss their job. Therefore, they adjusted with the circumstances whereas married, educated women of upper caste reported uncordial relations with men at workplace.

PERCEPTION OF WOMEN ABOUT THEIR STATUS AT WORKPLACE

An attempt has been made to study the kind of treatment these women get at their workplace by their male colleagues, superordinates and subordinates. Respondents were given eight statements to measure their perception about their status at workplace. The objective was to find out how working women rate their relationships with men at work place. Male domination and ill treatment as second class citizens are common problem the majority of Indian working women face. Another area in which women are at a disadvantaged in the workplace is through discrimination— Discrimination can be an uncomfortable situation for the women involved. There are two types of discrimination, indirect and direct, each affects women in a different way. Indirect discrimination might be a women being overlooked for a promotion, direct discrimination may include a woman being discharged from her employment because she is pregnant, or being excluded from after work group events. Another problem that women face is when men express their resentment and try to reassert control when they view women as economic competitors. Sexual harassment is closely linked to sex discrimination. Sexual discrimination forces women into lower paying jobs, and sexual harassment helps keep them there. One thing is clear, whether the problem is sexual harassment or sexual discrimination the problem continues to exist in the workplace, reminding women of their vulnerability and creating tension that make their jobs more difficult.

Working women in India constitute an important segment of our society. They have taken up work outside home both in formal as well as in informal sector and have proved their skill and worth almost in all the sphere of work. Yet cultural and structural constraints have hindered their path of progress. The notion of gender discrimination as perpetuated by patriarchy

TABLE 3.16
Perception of Women about their Status with Male Colleagues, Superordinates and Subordinates

Perception	*Colleagues*			*Superordinates*			*Subordinates*		
	Yes	*No*	*Un- decided*	*Yes*	*No*	*Un- decided*	*Yes*	*No*	*Un- decided*
(1)	*(2)*	*(3)*	*(4)*	*(5)*	*(6)*	*(7)*	*(8)*	*(9)*	*(10)*
Males treat as	92	98	10	97	94	9	45	140	8
their equals	46%	49%	5%	48.50%	47%	4.50%	23.30%	72.50%	4.20%
Males treat you	23	168	9	33	160	7	34	146	13
more intelligent	11.50%	84%	4.50%	16.50%	80%	3.50%	17.60%	75.60%	6.80%
Males treat you inferior	113	77	10	105	90	5	120	63	10
	56.50%	38.50%	5%	52.50%	45%	25%	62.10%	32.60%	5.18%
Males feel you get good	96	90	14	102	94	4	160	26	7
salary but perform less	48%	45%	7%	51.00%	47.00%	2%	82.90%	13.40%	3.70%
Males feel you can perform	99	93	8	100	92	8	19	162	12
your duties of your own	49.50%	46.50%	4%	50%	46%	4%	9.80%	83.90%	6.30%
Males treat you as	97	99	4	124	64	12	102	87	4
show piece in workplace	48.50%	49.50%	2%	62%	32%	6%	52.80%	45%	2.10%
Males feel you are of	100	94	6	124	64	12	89	98	6
easy moral	50%	47%	3%	62%	32%	6%	46.20%	50.70%	3.10%
Males feel you get promotions	92	102	6	88	110	6	160	29	4
because of being females	46%	51%	3%	44%	55%	3%	82.90%	15%	2.10%

* For colleagues N is 200, for superordinates N is 200, for subordinates N is 193, since 7 respondents did not have subordinates.

prohibits them to come at par with their male counterparts at workplace. Keeping this in mind, working women's perception about their status *vis-à-vis* their colleagues, superordinates and subordinates was evaluated.

Majority of the respondents, i.e. 72.5 percent felt that their subordinates feel that women are not equal to men. They reported that these men did not feel comfortable taking orders from female bosses. It is but natural that when a woman is not considered equal by males at workplace, then she can't be treated as more intelligent to males at workplace. Majority of the women felt that they were not treated as more intelligent to males at workplace, whether it was colleagues, superordinates or subordinates. There were 56.5 percent, 52.5 percent and 62.1 percent of the respondents who reported that they were treated inferior to males at workplace by their colleagues, superordinates or subordinates respectively. In Patriarchal society, like ours different prejudices against women exist. In spite of their capabilities, they are not treated good workers. It was also observed in the present study. Half of the respondents reported that their male colleagues and superordinates felt that females were poor performers. 82.9 percent of the respondents reported that their subordinates treated them as poor performers; 51.0 percent of the respondents reported that their superordinates and 48.0 percent mentioned that their colleagues felt that females were getting more salary than their performance. There were 107 respondents who were of the opinion that men in a subordinate position felt that females could never perform their duties of their own. 49.5 percent of the respondents reported that their colleagues and similar number of respondents mentioned that their superordinates felt that females could never perform their duties of their own. 62.0 percent reported that they were treated as show piece and of easy moral at the workplace by their male superordinates. Such results endorse the findings of various researchers who advocated that it is the superordinates who exploit female subordinates. Approximately 83.0 percent respondents held the view that their male subordinates did not pay them respect and misbehaved with them just because they were women.

They held the notion that females get promotions because they flaunt their sexuality.

Such results clearly indicate that working women are not given respect and status at the workplace which their male counterparts enjoy. Men doubt their capabilities as good worker. Men are not ready to accept females in superordinate positions. There was not much difference in the attitudes of male colleagues, superordinates and subordinates. These men view the female workers first as women and then as co-workers. The tendency of male employees to treat females at workplace as an object of sexuality results in discrimination and inequality. Further, Sex Role Theory and Power Theory have been found quite capable in the present context. Findings indicated that employment has not changed the status of women at workplace in the eyes of women respondents. Caplow (1973) reported that women's authority in workplace is still resented by men. This resistance comes out of a feeling that women are inferior and as such cannot perform their jobs as efficiently as men.

In this chapter an attempt was made to explore the work situation of the respondents undertaken for the study. Additionally, relationship with male colleagues, superordinates and subordinates was also explained. In the next chapter incidence, factors and perception related to problem of sexual harassment at workplace have been discussed.

4

Sexual Harassment

Sexual harassment at the workplace has remained one of the central concerns of the women's movement in India since the early 80's (Patel, 2002). Several women's groups came forward in support of a new concern about a variety of sexually violent acts against women, including sexual harassment. During the 1990s, the most controversial and brutal gang rape at the work place involved a Rajasthan State Government employee who tried to prevent child marriage as part of her duties as a worker of the Women Development Programme. The feudal patriarchs who were enraged by her (in their words: "a lowly woman from a poor and potter community") 'guts' decided to teach her a lesson and raped her repeatedly (Samhita, 2001). After an extremely humiliating legal battle in the Rajasthan High Court the rape survivor did not get justice and the rapists—"educated and upper caste affluent men"—were allowed to go free. This enraged a women's rights group called Vishakha that filed a public interest litigation in the Supreme Court of India (Combat Law, 2003).

Before 1997, women experiencing Sexual harassment at the workplace had to lodge a complaint under Section 354 of the Indian Penal Code that deals with the 'Criminal Assault of women to outrage women's modesty, and Section 509 that punishes an individual for using a 'word', gesture or act intended to insult the modesty of a woman'. These sections left the interpretation of outraging women's modesty to the discretion of the police officer.

In 1997, the Supreme Court passed a landmark judgment in the Vishakha Case laying down guidelines to be followed by establishments in dealing with complaints about sexual harassment. The Court stated that these guidelines were to be implemented until legislation is passed to deal with the issue (Mathew, 2002).

Pursuant to this, the Government of India requested the National Commission for Women (NCW) to draft the legislation. A number of issues were raised regarding the NCW draft, until, ultimately, a drafting committee was set-up to make a fresh draft several women's organizations and women lawyers collectively worked on the draft. The bill introduced in Parliament came to be known as the Sexual Harassment of women at the workplace (Prevention and Redressal) Bill, 2004. The bill provides for the prevention and redressal of sexual harassment of women at the workplace, or arising during and in the course of their employment and matters connected thereto, in keeping with the principles equality, freedom, life and liberty as enshrined in the Constitution of India, and as upheld by the Supreme Court in *Vishakha v. State of Rajasthan* (1997(7) SCC 323) and as reflected in the Convention on the Elimination of all Forms of Discrimination Against Women (CEDAW) which has been ratified by the Government of India. The cases of sexual harassment has decreased from 8.77 percent in 2003 to 6.48 percent in 2004 due to intervention of Government and follow-up action taken to fulfil the direction of the Supreme Court (Manohar, 2006).

One of the objectives of the present study was to explore working women's perception about sexual harassment, whether their understanding of sexual harassment coincides with Supreme Court's definition. The Supreme Court's definition has different components, i.e. unwelcome remarks, verbal and non-verbal conduct of sexual nature, sexually suggestive visual material, unwanted demands or requests and physical contact. In order to study working women's perception about sexual harassment, for all the five components, different statements were formulated (adapted from Fitzgerald, 1995). Each component was further divided into sub-parts. Part I contained three statements, Part II contained three statements, Part III contained three statements, Part IV contained four statements and Part V contained four statements. In this way, total 17 statements were formulated explaining the definition of sexual harassment. Further, each of these 17 statements were presented on 5 point Likert Scale, i.e. strongly agree, agree, undecided, disagree and strongly disagree. Distribution was done to know whether there were variations in the response of the respondents regarding each statement. The scores were coded to all these five responses. For 'Strongly agree' score '5' was coded, for 'agree' score '4' was given, for 'undecided' score '3' was given, for 'disagree' score '2' was given and for 'strongly disagree' score '1' was given.

The most important principle applied worldwide is that sexual harassment is conduct which is unwelcome and unwanted by the recipient. The intent of the harasser is not determinant. It is the recipient who determines whether the conduct is welcome or not. Most courts infer in this determination an element of reasonableness. Some acts are readily identifiable as 'sexual' harassment, for example, kissing, fondling of breasts, and physical contact with the genital areas, but many kinds of other physical, verbal or non-verbal conduct or display of objects or pictures can also be considered as sexual harassment. This varies according to cultural and social practices and the context in which it occurs. For example, in some cultures, physical touching upon greeting will be normal behaviour, whereas in other cultures it might be interpreted as insulting or a sexual advance. Behaviour which is acceptable between friends at work may be offensive if displayed by newcomers or outsiders. In addition, a whole range of acts which are not necessarily always of a 'sexual' nature, for example, placing an arm around another person's shoulders, stroking a person's hair, or comments about a person's look or body, may still constitute sexual harassment if the acts are unwelcome and unwanted. What is 'sexual' is not contingent upon what part of the body is involved. What is more crucial is the context within which an act is perpetrated and the character of the conduct. Sexually harassing conduct occurs when the sex or sexuality of the person and everything culturally related to it—from her/his body, to her/his manner of dress, to her/his intimate relations —is made the object or target of the conduct, as something desired to be obtained, or appropriated, or trivialized, whether through physical, verbal or other forms of conduct. Certain of these kinds of behaviour are inherently offensive: those involving physical violence or verbal aggression are the most obvious examples. But others mentioned above could, depending on the circumstances, be entirely harmless. Physical contact, for example, may be strongly objected to, tolerated or encouraged; jokes offensive to one person may be appreciated by another; the same comment may be welcomed, tolerated, or considered offensive depending on the relationship between the individuals involved, the context in which it was made, or even the tone in which it was delivered. Additionally, the kinds of behaviour considered sexually harassing appear to vary among different cultures.

The degree of physical contact tolerated between colleagues, for instance, may be more extensive in some cultures than others, while the range of topics considered appropriate to discuss in the workplace may also differ. It may, then, be neither possible nor desirable to draw up a comprehensive list of the range of behaviour which can be considered to be sexual harassment. Governments, employers' and workers' organizations, and other groups have been faced with the challenge of finding a way in which to identify sexual harassment when the conduct it covers may be unobjectionable in some circumstances and harmful in others.

Sexual harassment includes any unwelcome and sexually determined behaviour (whether directly or by implication). Any form of sexual attention becomes harassment when it is 'unwelcome'. Whether the perpetrator intentionally or unintentionally sexually harasses a person is not the issue. How the person at whom it is directed, receives that behaviour is crucial because of the subjective nature of sexual harassment. 'Unwelcome' is the key in defining sexual harassment. It is the impact and effect; the behaviour has on the recipient that will define the behaviour as sexual harassment. In addition to the five components of sexual harassment, there are some experiences of conduct which if unwelcome may constitute sexual harassment depending upon the totality of the circumstances including the severity of the conduct and its pervasiveness.

1. UNWELCOME REMARKS

In addition to the following instances unwelcome remarks may also include some other forms of sexual behaviour like sexual epithets, written or oral references to sexual conduct, comment or questions about an individuals social life or sexual life, deficiencies or prowess, comments about the victim's body or clothing, etc. For the purpose of analysis, perception on unwelcome remarks were tested on three statements, i.e. :

- When a man passes sexually explicit remarks or comments to a woman at workplace.
- When a man cracks jokes with sexual connotations to a woman at workplace.
- When a man passes sexist remarks on a woman at workplace.

All the respondents were asked to rate their perception of these three statements on five point scale ranging from strongly agree to strongly disagree. The responses to each statement were pre-coded as strongly agree, agree, undecided, disagree, strongly disagree to account for variations in the responses. To attain a cumulative position of individual different scores were allocated to their responses. The procedure adopted for assigning scores as well as dividing into five levels has been discussed in 'Appendix I'.

It was found there were 11 respondents who strongly disagreed and 39 respondents who disagreed that passing unwelcome remarks to a woman at workplace constitutes sexual harassment. Because, for them it was a part of their day-to-day life. They were used to such behaviour pattern, accepted as normal. There were 37 respondents who were in

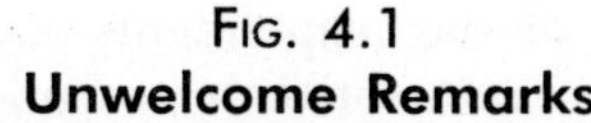

Fig. 4.1
Unwelcome Remarks

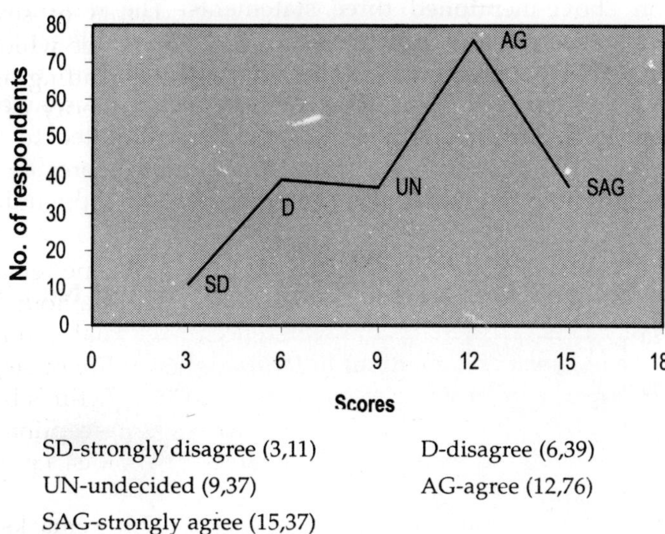

SD-strongly disagree (3,11) D-disagree (6,39)
UN-undecided (9,37) AG-agree (12,76)
SAG-strongly agree (15,37)

the 'undecided' category; they were not sure about the statements. There were 76 respondents who agreed and 37 respondents who strongly agreed that unwelcome remarks at workplace constituted sexual harassment.

2. VERBAL AND NON-VERBAL CONDUCT OF SEXUAL NATURE

It includes unwelcome leering, whistling, suggestive or insulting comments, oral or written requests or demands for dates or sex etc. For the purpose of analysis, perception of respondents on verbal and non-verbal conduct of sexual nature were framed in three statements, i.e. :

- When a man at workplace stares at a woman to make her uncomfortable.
- When a man makes offensive gestures in front of a woman at workplace.
- When a man makes kissing sounds to a woman at workplace.

The responses of the respondents regarding verbal and non-verbal conduct of sexual nature at workplace were worked out on above-mentioned three statements. The responses to each statement were arranged on five point Likert Scale ranging from 'strongly agree' to 'strongly disagree' through 'agree', 'undecided' and 'disagree'. To attain a cumulative position of individual different scores were allocated to their responses. The procedure adopted for assigning scores as well as dividing into five levels has been discussed in 'Appendix II'.

FIG. 4.2

Verbal and Non-verbal Conduct of Sexual Nature

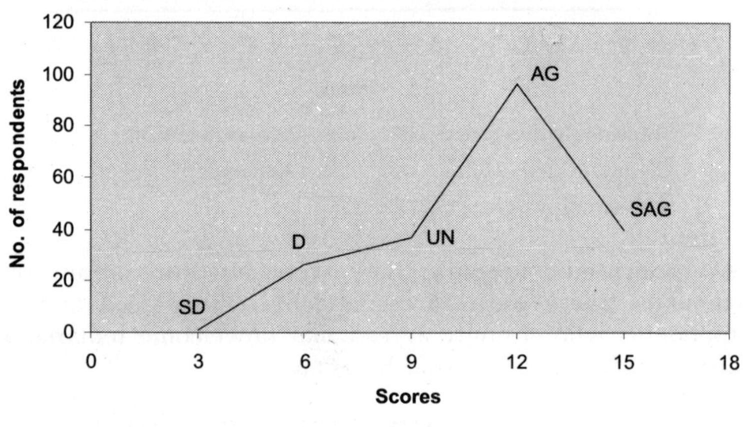

SD-strongly disagree (3,1) D-disagree (6,26)
UN-undecided (9,37) AG-agree (12,96)
SAG-strongly agree (15,40)

Distribution indicates that 26 respondents disagreed with the statements and only 1 respondent strongly disagreed with the statements, they did not consider Verbal and non-verbal conduct of sexual nature as sexual harassment. Most of these women faced harassment of this nature everyday in their lives. As a consequence they developed tolerance for it and did not perceived it as harassment. There were 37 respondents who remained undecided. They could not give any response. There were 96 respondents, who agreed that these statements resulted in sexual harassment. There were 40 respondents who strongly agreed with the statements. They perceived any act of Verbal and non-verbal conduct of sexual nature as sexual harassment.

3. SEXUALLY SUGGESTIVE VISUAL MATERIAL

It includes displaying sexually suggestive objects, pictures, displaying body parts, etc. Sexually suggestive visual material constituted three statements for the purpose of analysis, i.e.:

- When a man shows sexually explicit books/ magazines/printed matter to a woman at workplace.
- When a man shows sexually explicit cartoons/ posters/calendars to female worker at workplace.
- When a man shows pornographic e-mails/sms/ screen savers to a female worker at workplace.

In order to determine the perception of the respondents on definition of sexual harassment on sexually suggestive visual material three statements were made. The responses to each statement were arranged on five point Likert Scale ranging from 'strongly agree' to 'strongly disagree' through 'agree', 'undecided' and 'disagree'. According to the responses given, each statement was coded. The procedure adopted for assigning scores as well as dividing into five levels has been discussed in 'Appendix III'.

Results indicate that 10 respondents disagreed with the statements and only 1 respondent strongly disagreed with the statements. They did not perceive showing sexually suggestive visual material as sexual harassment. They were of the view that media has been portraying the negative picture of women. They blamed women for this negative image. Men only show which is already available. In such a situation if men show pornographic material they don't consider it harassment. 39 respondents were not clear about the statements, they neither agreed nor disagreed. There were 150 respondents who perceived showing sexually suggestive visual material as sexual harassment, i.e. 124 respondents agreed and 26 respondents strongly agreed with statements.

FIG. 4.3
Sexually Suggestive Visual Material

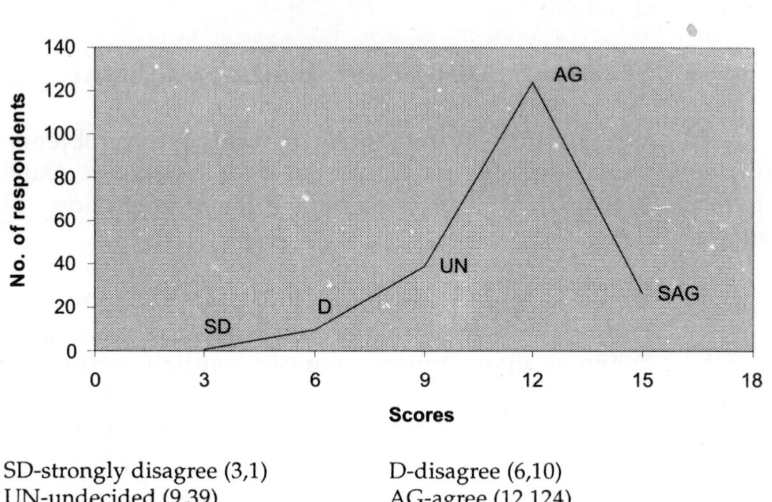

SD-strongly disagree (3,1)
D-disagree (6,10)
UN-undecided (9,39)
AG-agree (12,124)
SAG-strongly agree (15,26)

4. UNWELCOME DEMANDS OR REQUESTS

The laws against sexual harassment are violated when "submission to such conduct is made either explicitly or implicitly in terms or conditions of employment." This refers to what is sometimes called quid pro quo sexual harassment, in which a victim's hire, job security, pay, receipt of benefits, or status depends on her response to a superior's sexual overtures, comments, or actions. The *quid pro quo* may be direct, as when a superior explicitly demands sexual favors and threatens firing if the demands are not met, or it may be indirect, as when a superior suggests that employment success depends on "personality" or "friendship" rather than competence. For the purpose of analysis, it constituted four statements, i.e.:

- When a man demands or requests for sexual favours in return of payment of wages from a female employee at workplace.

- When a man demands for sexual favours from a female employee at workplace and makes it a condition for employment.
- When a man demands for sexual favours from a female employee at workplace and makes it a condition for increment.
- When a man demands for sexual favours from a female employee at workplace and makes it a condition for promotion.

The perception of the respondents regarding unwelcome demands or requests were worked out with four statements. The responses to each statement were arranged on five point Likert Scale ranging from 'strongly agree' to 'strongly disagree' through 'agree', 'undecided' and 'disagree'. According to the response given each statement was coded. The procedure adopted for assigning scores as well as dividing into five levels has been discussed in 'Appendix IV'.

FIG. 4.4
Unwelcome Demands

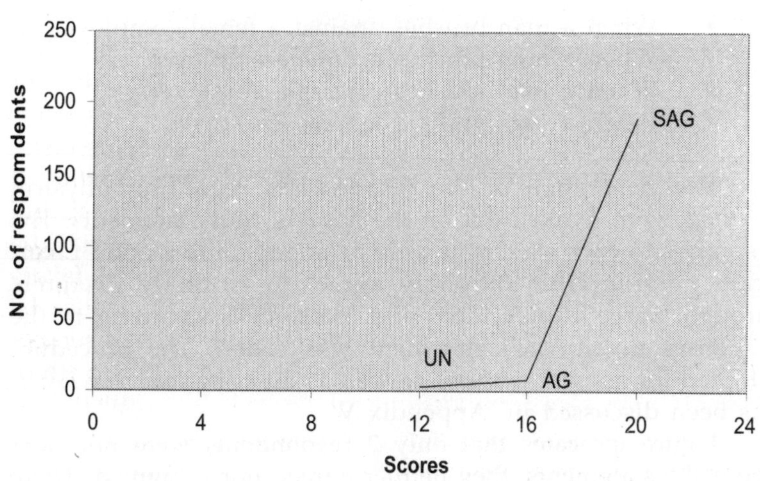

UN-Undecided (12,2) AG-agree (16,7)

SAC-strongly agree (20,191)

Figure clearly indicates that only 2 respondents were not clear about the statements whereas 7 respondents agreed with the statements and perceived unwelcome demands or requests as sexual harassment. Majority of the respondents, i.e. 191 cases strongly agreed with the statements and perceived unwelcome demands or requests as sexual harassment.

In other words, there were only 2 respondents who were not clear about the statements. Rest of 198 respondents perceived unwelcome demands as sexual harassment. For them, sexual favours in return of wages, employment, increment and promotion is something illegal and unbearable and they perceived it as sexual harassment.

5. PHYSICAL CONTACTS

In addition to the following acts it may also include patting, blocking the victim's path, standing very close to the victim, pulling clothing, etc. To find out the perception of respondents on 'Physical contacts' four statements were used, i.e.

- When a man brushes against a female employee
- When a man pinches a female employee
- When a man touches a female employee
- When a man grabs a female employee.

The perception of the respondents regarding physical contacts were worked out on the basis of four statements. The responses to each statement were arranged on five point Likert Scale ranging from 'strongly agree' to 'strongly disagree' through 'agree', 'undecided' and 'disagree'. According to the responses given, each statement was coded. The procedure adopted for assigning scores as well as dividing into five levels has been discussed in 'Appendix V'.

Figure indicates that only 2 respondents were not clear about the statements, they neither agreed nor disagreed. There were 8 respondents who agreed with the statements and considered it as sexual harassment. Majority of the respondents, i.e. 190 strongly agreed with the statements and considered physical contacts as sexual harassment. Out of 200

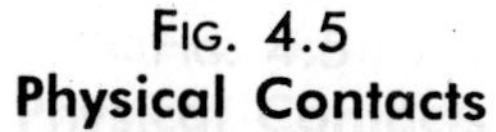

Fig. 4.5
Physical Contacts

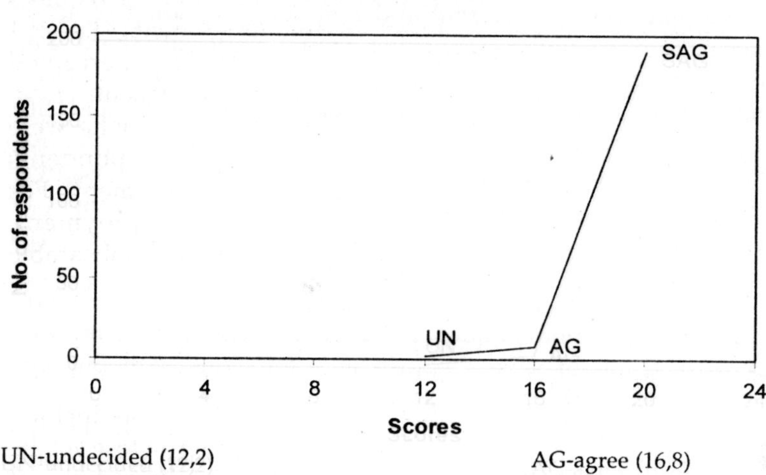

UN-undecided (12,2) AG-agree (16,8)

SAG-strongly agree (20,190)

respondents there were only 2 respondents who were not clear about the statements. Rest of the 198 respondents considered physical contacts at workplace as sexual harassment. There can be hardly any woman who does not consider physical contacts as sexual harassment as physical contact is the severe form of sexual harassment.

Thus, it was observed that there were variations among the responses of the respondents regarding five components that are basis of the Supreme Court's definition of sexual harassment. As, the statements varied from mild to severe form, responses of the respondents also varied. There were more respondents with disagree response for the first component, i.e. unwelcome remarks and reduced gradually in the second component, i.e. verbal and non verbal conduct of sexual nature, few respondents disagreed with the third component, i.e. sexually visual material and there were no respondents who disagreed with the fourth and fifth components, i.e. unwelcome demands or requests and physical contacts. It clearly shows that respondents who did not perceive unwelcome remarks, verbal and non-verbal conduct of sexual nature as sexual harassment, but perceived severe forms of sexual harassment as sexual harassment. It has been noticed that with regard to first three components namely unwelcome remarks, verbal and non-verbal conduct of sexual nature and sexually suggestive visual material, there were some respondents who did not perceive it as sexual harassment as part of various reasons. For fourth and fifth components namely unwelcome demands and physical contacts, there were hardly any respondents who disagreed with statements. Such results clearly indicate that there is no acceptance for physical harassment whereas with remarks, pornography, some disagreement occurred.

Further, an attempt was made to explore working women's perception about sexual harassment, whether their understanding of sexual harassment coincides with Supreme Court's definition of sexual harassment. Sexual harassment scores were calculated by taking the scores of all the five components, i.e. 17 statements covering all the components. The responses to each statement were arranged on five point Likert scale ranging from 'strongly agree' to 'strongly disagree' through 'agree', 'undecided' and 'disagree'. According to the response given, each statement was coded. The scores should have ranged from 17 to 85. However, the scores of the respondents ranged from 50 to 85. Such distribution clearly indicates that majority of the respondents were in agreement with the Supreme Court's definition of sexual harassment. (The procedure adopted for assigning scores as well as dividing into three levels has been discussed in 'Appendix VI'). For the purpose of analysis perception of the respondents on the sexual harassment has been divided into three categories, i.e. Almost Agree, Strongly Agree and Certain.

Table 4.1 shows the perception of 200 respondents on sexual harassment. There were 56 respondents who did not hold strong opinion about sexual harassment on the basis of statements given on all the main components of harassment. However, they almost agreed with the definition. There were 48 respondents who strongly agreed with the statements measuring sexual harassment. There were 96 respondents, i.e. 48.0 percent who were certain that these statements counted for sexual harassment. Findings about perception of the

TABLE 4.1
Distribution of the Respondents on their Perception of Sexual Harassment

Perception on sexual harassment	*Scores*	*Frequency*	*Percentage*
Almost Agree	50-67	56	28.0
Strongly Agree	68-71	48	24.0
Certain	72-85	96	48.0
Total		200	100.0

respondents clearly indicate that the Supreme Court's definition coincides with perception of the respondents in the present study.

To get the holistic picture of respondents' perception on sexual harassment, it is important to study perception of respondents on definition of sexual harassment in relation with age, marital status, caste, religion, education and occupation.

PERCEPTION OF SEXUAL HARASSMENT ACCORDING TO AGE OF THE RESPONDENTS

A few researcher states that the perception of men and women not only differed but women's perception of sexual harassment also varied with age. Older women find physical touch unacceptable while the younger women are less formal in their social interactions with male colleagues (Tang, 2000; The Lawyers' Collective, 2001).

In another study it is indicated that while older women tend to put up with sexual harassment, younger generations of women show resistance to sexual harassment practices because of increased awareness and the need to assert a sense of self dignity (Wijayatilake and Zackariya, 2000). An attempt has been made to understand the perception of respondents according to age.

Table clearly indicates that 57.1 percent respondents of below 25 years age group; 49.6 percent respondents in the age group of 25-35 years and 37.5 percent respondents of above 35

TABLE 4.2
Age and Perception Regarding Sexual Harassment

Age	*Sexual Harassment*			*Total*
	Almost Agree	*Strongly Agree*	*Certain*	
Below 25 Yrs.	11 31.4%	4 11.4%	20 57.1%	35
25-35 Yrs.	31 26.5%	28 23.9%	58 49.6%	117
Above 35 Yrs.	14 29.2%	16 33.3%	18 37.5%	48
Total	56 28.0%	48 24.0%	96 48.0%	200

years age group were certain about the definition of sexual harassment. Thus, irrespective of the age group, majority of the respondents perceived sexual harassment in consensus with the Supreme Court's definition. Results do not show any variation in the perception of the respondents according to age.

PERCEPTION OF SEXUAL HARASSMENT ACCORDING TO MARITAL STATUS OF THE RESPONDENTS

It was assumed that perception of the respondents about sexual harassment is influenced by their marital status. Married women have support of their husbands, thus they are ready to take action against their perpetrators.

Keeping this in mind an attempt has been made to find perception of sexual harassment according to the marital status of the respondents. There were 50.0 percent respondents who were single, i.e. not staying with their partners perceived sexual harassment as mentioned in the Supreme Court's definition. Similarly, 45.7 percent of married respondents were certain about their perception of sexual harassment. There was not much difference in the perception of single and married respondents. However, majority of single respondents perceived sexual harassment in consensus with the Supreme Court's definition.

Table 4.3
Marital Status and Perception Regarding Sexual Harassment

Marital Status	*Sexual Harassment*			*Total*
	Almost Agree	*Strongly Agree*	*Certain*	
Single at Present	29 27.4%	24 22.6%	53 50.0%	106
Married	27 28.7%	24 25.5%	43 45.7%	94
Total	56 28.0%	48 24.0%	96 48.0%	200

PERCEPTION OF SEXUAL HARASSMENT ACCORDING TO CASTE OF THE RESPONDENTS

An attempt has been made to find out the role of caste in influencing the respondents' perception about sexual harassment.

Table 4.4
Caste and Perception Regarding Sexual Harassment

Caste	*Sexual Harassment*			*Total*
	Almost Agree	*Strongly Agree*	*Certain*	
Upper	33 29.2%	24 21.2%	56 49.6%	113
Intermediate	17 34.7%	12 24.5%	20 40.8%	49
Lower	6 5.8%	12 31.6%	20 52.6%	38
Total	56 28.0%	48 24.0%	96 48.0%	200

It is clear from the above table that 49.6 percent respondents of the upper caste, 40.8 percent respondents of the intermediate caste group and 52.6 percent respondents of the lower caste were certain about the definition of sexual harassment. Thus, irrespective of the caste, majority of the respondents perceived sexual harassment the way it has been defined by the Supreme Court's definition. Results showed no influence of caste background on the perception of respondents on sexual harassment.

PERCEPTION OF SEXUAL HARASSMENT ACCORDING TO RELIGION OF THE RESPONDENTS

Religious affiliations can also influence the perception of the respondents. An attempt has been made to find out the role of religion in influencing the perception of the respondents.

TABLE 4.5
Religion and Perception Regarding Sexual Harassment

Religion	*Sexual Harassment*			*Total*
	Almost Agree	*Strongly Agree*	*Certain*	
Hindus	44 29.3%	37 24.7%	69 46.0%	150
Sikhs	11 24.4%	11 24.4%	23 51.1%	45
Muslims	1 50.0%	0 0.0%	1 50.0%	2
Christians	0 0.0%	0 0.0%	3 100.0%	3
Total	56 28.0%	48 24.0%	96 48.0%	200

There were 46.0 percent Hindus, 51.1 percent Sikhs, 50.0 percent Muslims and 100.0 percent Christian respondents were certain about the Supreme Court's definition of sexual harassment. Results showed no influence of the religion in colouring the perception of the respondents on sexual harassment.

PERCEPTION OF SEXUAL HARASSMENT ACCORDING TO EDUCATION OF THE RESPONDENTS

Role of education in enhancing the knowledge of the person cannot be denied. To know, how illiterate and educated respondents perceived sexual harassment, Table 4.6 was formulated. It was assumed that educated women will be more aware of the problem of sexual harassment and will have clear perception about the definition of sexual harassment.

TABLE 4.6
Education and Perception Regarding Sexual Harassment

Education	*Sexual Harassment*			*Total*
	Almost Agree	*Strongly Agree*	*Certain*	
Illiterate	13	11	14	38
	34.20%	28.90%	36.80%	
Educated	43	37	82	162
	26.5%	22.8%	50.6%	
Total	56	48	96	200
	28.0%	24.0%	48.0%	

Results do not show much difference in the perception of illiterates. 36.8 percent illiterate respondents were certain about the definition of sexual harassment and 34.2 percent respondents almost agreed with definition of sexual harassment. However, among the educated respondents, 50.6 percent respondents were certain that their definition coincides with the Supreme Court's definition of sexual harassment and 26.5 percent almost agreed with the definition. Findings indicated that more educated women's perception of sexual harassment was congruent to the Supreme Court's definition as compared to uneducated women. Thus, it can be concluded that educated women were more aware of their rights and had awareness regarding sexual harassment at workplace.

PERCEPTION OF SEXUAL HARASSMENT ACCORDING TO OCCUPATION OF THE RESPONDENTS

Occupation is an important indicator of a persons' position in society. It is believed that higher the education one has, the higher the occupation one holds and higher the prestige he gets in the society. An attempt has been made to find out whether women's perception is influenced by their occupational status.

TABLE 4.7
Occupation and Perception on Sexual Harassment

Occupation	*Sexual Harassment*			*Total*
	Almost Agree	*Strongly Agree*	*Certain*	
Upper	20 28.6%	16 22.9%	34 48.6%	70
Middle	21 23.6%	20 22.5%	48 53.9%	89
Lower	15 36.6%	12 29.3%	14 34.1%	41
Total	56 28.0%	48 24.0%	96 48.0%	200

There were 48.6 percent respondents in the occupations of higher prestige, 53.9 percent respondents in middle level occupations and 34.1 percent respondents of lower level of occupations who were certain about the Supreme Court's definition of sexual harassment. Their perception coincided with it. There were 36.6 percent of the respondents who almost agreed with the definition but majority of them belonged to occupations of lower prestige. Results indicated that wome belonging to lower level of occupation are doubly exploited, one because of their sex and other because of their poor economic status. These women having faced many atrocities become immune to extremities. As a result their perception about sexual harassment is not very severe.

PROBLEMS THAT WORKING WOMEN FACED AT WORKPLACE

With more and more women becoming wage earners, it is imperative to study the problems faced by them at their workplaces so as to provide remedial measures for improvement of their condition and reduce their problems. At workplace, women have to deal with male colleagues, superordinates as well as subordinates. They face different kinds of problems at workplace. Rani (1976), Kapur (1974) focused on the "role conflict" in working women. Working women were asked to report the problems they faced at workplace.

TABLE 4.8
Distribution of Respondents According to Workplace Problems

Problems	*Frequency*	*Percent*
Economic	10	5.0
Overtime	10	5.0
Discrimination	24	12.0
Sexual Harassment	138	69.0
Any Other	18	9.0
Total	200	100.0

It is clear from the Table 4.8 that majority of the respondents i.e. 69.0 percent reported that sexual harassment was the major problem at the workplace. 12.0 percent respondents reported they were discriminated at workplace. They were not promoted even when they were qualified. There were 10 respondents who reported that they were paid according to work. They did not get enhancement in their wages and this was a problematic situation. There were 10 respondents who reported that they had to work overtime which disturbed their family life and it was not comfortable for them to work late hours. There were 18 respondents who referred to different problems like adjustment problem of work environment, wage discrimination, strict working environment, etc.

WITNESSED HARASSMENT OF OTHER FEMALE WORKERS AT WORKPLACE

It was not easy to gather information on sexual harassment at workplace. In order to develop rapport with respondents, they were first asked to report whether they had witnessed any female getting sexually harassed at their workplace. Further such information will help in knowing the extent of the problem, which is quite rampant according to various studies (Dalal, 2003; ILO, 2001).

TABLE 4.9

Distribution of Respondents who Witnessed Sexual Harassment of Other Females at their Workplace

Sexual Harassment of other females	*Frequency*	*Percent*
Yes	146	73.0
No	54	27.0
Total	200	100.0

There were 73.0 percent of the respondents who witnessed sexual harassment of other female workers at their workplace. 27.0 percent of the respondents denied being witness to such episodes at their workplace. Such results clearly indicate that for a large number of women harassment at workplace is a frequently occurring phenomenon.

Those women who witnessed sexual harassment of other women at the workplace were further asked to mention their

TABLE 4.10
Reactions to Sexual Harassment of Other Females at Workplace by the Respondents

Reactions	*Frequency*	*Percent*
Mute Spectator	46	31.5
Sympathized her	42	28.8
Motivated for action	58	39.7
Total	146	100.0

* 54 respondents did not witness sexual harassment of other females in workplace.

reactions about the episodes. It was observed that 39.7 percent of the respondents motivated the victim to take action. They encouraged the victims to report the harassment to higher official. They instigated the victims to punish the perpetrators of harassment. 31.5 percent of the respondents reported that they remained mute spectators, as they never wanted to get involved in others affairs'. A few respondents reported that they were not aware of the facts; therefore they decided to remain neutral. 28.8 percent of the respondents sympathized with the victims as they felt that they could not help victims otherwise so they only consoled them. None of the respondent filed complaint against the perpetrator on behalf of the victim.

OPINION ON THE ACTION VICTIM SHOULD HAVE TAKEN

For the present study it was important to find out that what action the victims according to the respondents should take.

Results show that majority of the respondents, i.e. 67.5 percent favoured taking active action like complaining to the higher authorities, going to NGO's, filing police complaints etc. 32.5 percent of the respondents favoured taking passive actions like keeping mum, ignoring the problem or leaving the job. Such findings indicated that despite the legislations favouring

TABLE 4.11
Opinion on the Action Victim should have Taken

Actions	*Frequency*	*Percent*
Passive	65	32.5
Active	135	67.5
Total	200	100.0

working women, women were not in favour of coming out openly and taking strict measures against their perpetrators.

OPINION ON THE PUNISHMENT TO BE GIVEN TO THE PERPETRATOR

It has been found that majority of the respondents were in favour of taking active action against the harasser. For the present study, it is also important to know the opinion of the respondents on the type of punishment that should be given to the perpetrators.

TABLE 4.12
Opinion on the Punishment to be Given to the Perpetrator

Punishment	*Frequency*	*Percent*
Public Humiliation	63	31.5
Physical Punishment	47	23.5
Police Action	69	34.5
Suspension	21	10.5
Total	200	100.0

Majority of the respondents, i.e. 34.5 percent were in favour of taking rigorous action, i.e. police action. 31.5 percent of the respondents were in favour of punishment in the form of public humiliation. 23.5 percent of the respondents reported that perpetrator should be given physical punishment either by the victims or the family members. There were 10.5 percent respondents who reported that perpetrator should be suspended from his services in order to teach him a lesson. They did not want their services to be terminated, as they wanted to give them another chance.

WOMEN THAT ARE PRONE TO SEXUAL HARASSMENT

An attempt has been made to find out which women were prone to sexual harassment at workplace according to women themselves.

TABLE 4.13
Distribution of Women Prone to Sexual Harassment

Which women are sexually harassed	*Frequency*	*Percent*
Physically attractive	23	11.5
Economically needy	46	23.0
Weak personality	45	22.5
Weak family background	18	9.0
High qualification	17	8.5
Sexualized workplace environment	51	25.5
Total	200	100.0

Majority of the respondents, i.e. 25.5 percent considered workplace environment as the main factor for sexual harassment of women. Workplace environment referred to a situation where women were supervised by men, working in a highly sexualized fields (male to female ratio in high), working at odd hours, etc. 23.0 percent of the respondents were of the view that chances of sexual harassment were more among the economically needy women. Their economic necessity is known to the perpetrator and he exploits that. 22.5 percent of the respondents considered weak personality of the victim in the sense that they were afraid of reprisals; women blamed themselves as responsible factor for sexual harassment at workplace. 11.5 percent of the respondents believed that physical attributes, i.e. young, beautiful women were more likely to be harassed. 9.0 percent of the respondents considered weak family background like no family support, member of minority community, etc. as main factors for sexual harassment. 8.5 percent of the respondents believed that women with high qualification were likely to be harassed because they were treated as a threat to men at the workplace.

REASONS FOR EXISTENCE OF SEXUAL HARASSMENT IN THE SOCIETY

Findings of the present study indicated that the problem of sexual harassment exists rampantly at the workplace. An attempt was made to find out the main reasons for existence and continuation of problem in society.

TABLE 4.14
Reasons for Existence of Sexual Harassment in the Society

Reasons for existence of Sexual Harassment	*Frequency*	*Percent*
Underreporting	63	31.5
Weak Legal System	47	23.5
Social Stigma	52	26.0
Negative image of women in Media	18	9.0
Stigma and poor legislations	20	10.0
Total	200	100.0

Though Government of India has come out with legislation on sexual harassment, still it continues unabated. The respondents were asked to report the reasons for its existence in the society. 31.5 percent of the respondents were of the view that sexual harassment continued to exist because cases go unreported. According to them the majority of the victims are afraid of reprisals resulting in underreporting. 26.0

percent of the respondents felt that since stigma gets attached to women who report that matter. Women do not report the matter and men continue with harassment. There were 47 respondents who blamed weak legal system responsible for existence of sexual harassment. They were of the view that in India there is no dearth of legislation, but delayed justice and low conviction rate breaks the morale of the women and they prefer not to complain. As a consequence problem continued to exist. 10.0 percent of the respondents blamed both social stigma and poor legislations for existence of sexual harassment. 9.0 percent of the respondents blamed media for portraying negative image of the women as a consequence crime against women has increased.

SEXUAL HARASSMENT OF THE RESPONDENTS BY MALE COLLEAGUES, SUPERORDINATES AND SUBORDINATES

When sexual harassment is conceptualized as the exercise of power, it is generally understood that it is the male superior who perpetrates it against a female holding a lower level position. It has been found that most of the sexual harassment of women at workplace comes from their superordinates. Sometimes male co-workers and subordinates are also involved in harassment. Sexual harassment is typically perpetuated by a person in a position of authority. In a study

TABLE 4.15

Distribution of Respondents According to their Sexual Harassment by Male Colleagues, Superordinates and Subordinates

Response	*Colleagues*	*Superordinates*	*Subordinates*
Yes	54 27.0%	68 34.0%	20 10.0%
No	146 73.0%	132 66.0%	180 90.0%
Total	200	200	200

done it has been indicated that 90.0 percent of women are harassed by their superior, 7.0 percent by fellow workers and 3.0 percent by subordinates (Zaitun, 2001).

Table 4.15 shows that maximum sexual harassment of women in the present study comes from supervisors, i.e. 34.0 percent, followed by colleagues, i.e. 27.0 percent. Least sexual harassment of women comes from subordinates, i.e. 10.0 percent. It makes clear that men who are in power positions also hold the authority of harassing women. Results support the power theory that superiors harass because they have the power.

FIG. 4.6
Sexual Harassment by Male Colleagues, Superordinates, Subordinates

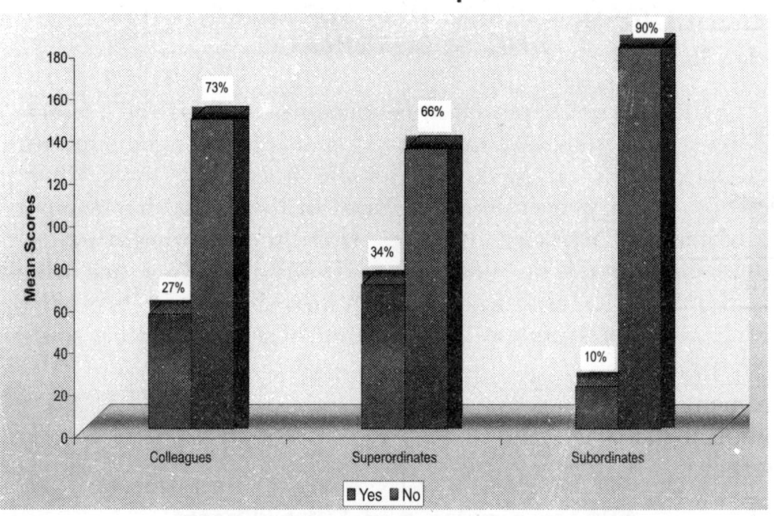

AGE OF THE RESPONDENTS AND SEXUAL HARASSMENT BY MALE COLLEAGUES, SUPERORDINATES AND SUBORDINATES

An attempt was made to find out relationship between age and sexual harassment by male colleagues, superordinates and subordinates. Previous research suggests that since younger women constitute a less powerful group and tend to be in lower levels of the organization, they may be particularly susceptible to being sexually harassed (Farley, 1983; Merit Systems Protection Board, 1981, 1988, 1995). Fain and Anderton (1987) found that maximum harassment of individuals was in the age group of 16 and 34 years and harassment declined with increasing age.

TABLE 4.16

Age of the Respondents and Sexual Harassment by Male Colleagues, Superordinates and Subordinates

Age	*Colleagues*		*Superordinates*		*Subordinates*	
	Yes	*No*	*Yes*	*No*	*Yes*	*No*
(1)	(2)	(3)	(4)	(5)	(6)	(7)
Below 25	8 14.8%	27 18.4%	12 17.6%	23 17.4%	3 15.0%	32 17.8%
25-35	36 66.6%	81 55.4%	36 52.9%	81 61.5%	15 75.0%	102 0.6%
35-45	10 18.6%	38 26.2%	20 29.5%	28 21.1%	2 10.0%	46 25.6%
Total	54	146	68	132	20	180

Table 4.16 shows that maximum sexual harassment of women at workplace by male colleagues, superordinates and subordinates was among the age group of 25-35 years, i.e. 66.6 percent by male colleagues, 52.9 percent by male superordinates and 75.0 percent by subordinates. It was mainly because younger women were new in profession, holds low occupational level, usually unmarried, thus constituting a less powerful group. Findings endorse the results of the research that reported that women upto the age of 35 years were more vulnerable to sexual harassment. However, sexual harassment in the younger age group did not emerge as most vulnerable group.

MARITAL STATUS OF THE RESPONDENTS AND THEIR SEXUAL HARASSMENT BY MALE COLLEAGUES, SUPERORDINATES AND SUBORDINATES.

Table 4.17 presents the relationship between marital status and sexual harassment by male colleagues, superordinates and subordinates. Marital status of a woman may be an important moderator for the occurrence of sexual harassment. The U.S. Merit System Protection Board (1981, 1988) reported that sexual harassment was less among married women than unmarried women.

TABLE 4.17
Marital Status of the Respondents and Sexual Harassment by Male Colleagues, Superordinates and Subordinates

Marital Status	*Colleagues*		*Superordinates*		*Subordinates*	
	Yes	*No*	*Yes*	*No*	*Yes*	*No*
(1)	(2)	(3)	(4)	(5)	(6)	(7)
Single at present	23 42.6%	83 56.8%	27 39.7%	79 59.8%	12 60.0%	94 52.2%
Married	31 57.4%	63 43.2%	41 60.3%	53 40.2%	8 40.0%	86 47.8%
Total	54	146	68	132	20	180

* The category 'single at present' included respondents who were unmarried, widowed, separated or divorced.

Table 4.17 indicates that maximum sexual harassment by male colleagues and superordinates was among married women, i.e. 57.4 percent and 60.3 percent whereas the maximum sexual harassment by male subordinates was among single women, i.e. 55.0 percent. It may be because superordinates can harass women of any marital status by using their position. Subordinates harassed women who were single because men in lower position to women were not ready to take commands from female in spite of the fact occupationally women occupied higher position they continued to occupy lower position in the social ladder.

EDUCATION OF THE RESPONDENTS AND SEXUAL HARASSMENT BY MALE COLLEAGUES, SUPERORDINATES AND SUBORDINATES

An attempt has been made to find out the relationship between education and sexual harassment by male colleagues, superordinates and subordinates. Highly educated women may be more sensitive to sexual harassment behaviours and protective of their rights. Fain and Anderton (1987) indicated that harassment was more likely to occur for women who had some technical or college education, and less likely to occur for those with college degrees or graduate education. Higher levels of education of women could dampen the tendency of men to be sexually aggressive.

TABLE 4.18

Education of the Respondents and Sexual Harassment by Male Colleagues, Superordinates and Subordinates

Education	*Colleagues*		*Superordinates*		*Subordinates*	
	Yes	*No*	*Yes*	*No*	*Yes*	*No*
(1)	*(2)*	*(3)*	*(4)*	*(5)*	*(6)*	*(7)*
Illiterate	14 25.9%	24 16.4%	14 20.6%	24 18.2%	2 10.0%	36 20.0%
High School	10 18.5%	15 10.3%	6 8.8%	19 14.4%	5 25.0%	20 11.1%
Graduate	14 25.9%	53 36.3%	23 33.8%	44 33.3%	3 15.0%	60 36.6%
Post-graduate and above	16 29.6%	54 37.0%	25 36.8%	45 34.1%	10 50.0%	60 33.3%
Total	54	146	68	132	20	180

Table 4.18 indicates that maximum sexual harassment of women by male colleagues, superordinates and subordinates

was more among highly educated women, i.e. 29.6 percent by male colleagues, 36.8 percent by male superordinates and 50.0 percent by male subordinates. The difference in the harassment and different educational level was not much. Results showed that harassment was also high among illiterate women. Results don't endorse the findings of Fair and Anderton.

OCCUPATION OF RESPONDENTS AND THEIR SEXUAL HARASSMENT BY MALE COLLEAGUES, SUPERORDINATES AND SUBORDINATES

An attempt has been made to find out the relationship between occupation and sexual harassment by male colleagues, superordinates and subordinates. Occupational status of women is considered to be an important factor for the prevalence of sexual harassment.

TABLE 4.19

Occupation of the Respondents and Sexual Harassment by Male Colleagues, Superordinates and Subordinates

Caste	*Colleagues*		*Superordinates*		*Subordinates*	
	Yes	*No*	*Yes*	*No*	*Yes*	*No*
(1)	*(2)*	*(3)*	*(4)*	*(5)*	*(6)*	*(7)*
Upper	16 29.6%	54 37.0%	29 42.6%	41 31.1%	8 40.0%	62 34.4%
Middle	21 38.9%	68 46.6%	25 36.8%	64 48.5%	10 50.0%	79 43.9%
Lower	17 31.5%	24 16.4%	14 20.6%	27 20.5%	2 10.0%	39 21.7%
Total	54	146	68	132	20	180

It has been found that maximum harassment by male colleagues and subordinates was among middle occupational level women and the percentage was 38.9 percent and 50.0 percent respectively. It was because colleagues and subordinates would hesitate to harass the women of upper occupational level. Maximum harassment by male superordinates was found to be among the women of upper occupational level because superordinates hold the power at workplace.

In the present study, there were four such respondents, who were harassed by their male colleagues, superordinates as well as by the subordinates in the same workplace. Among these respondents, two respondents were in 25-35 years age group and remaining two were in 35-45 years age group. Three respondents were Post Graduate and one was Graduate. Regarding marital status, two respondents were single and two respondents were married. Regarding occupation, three respondents were of middle occupational level and one respondent was of upper occupational level.

HOW SEXUALLY HARASSED WOMEN SOLVED THEIR PROBLEM

Results indicate that majority of the respondents faced sexual harassment at the workplace. It becomes essential to know how these harassed women tried to solve their problem. Different researchers have indicated that fear of loosing jobs discouraged victims to take any action against their perpetrators (Coles, 1986; Sandroff, 1992; Srivastava, 2004; Terpstra & Cook, 1985). Srivastava (2004) has given some main causes of non-reporting of sexual harassment, i.e. fear of losing

TABLE 4.20

How Respondents Solved their Problems

Solution of the problem	*Frequency*	*Percent*
Ignored the problem	26	18.8
Shared with family members	30	21.7
Shared with friends and office staff	44	31.8
Complained to higher official	38	27.7
Total	138	100.0

* 62 respondents did not face sexual harassment at workplace.

job, fear of not getting promotions, fear of victimization by the employer, fear of being neglected by her family members and among others, slow to improve the situation.

Results show that majority of women who were harassed at the workplace, i.e. 31.8 percent shared their problem with friends and office staff. 38.0 percent respondents reported that they complained to the higher officials. 21.7 percent respondents shared their problem with their family members only. There were 26.0 respondents who reported that in spite of the fact they were harassed they ignored their problem as they believed that their harassers would mend their ways.

Results clearly indicated that although 39.7 percent of women suggested strict action against the perpetrators. There was less number of women who complained to authorities when they themselves became victims of harassment. Most harassed working women were hesitant to complain about their plight. Victims still prefer to bear it in silence than to lodge a complaint. This stems from the fear of losing the job itself, getting transferred or inviting other reprisals, etc. None of the women approached the police.

WHOM RESPONDENTS BLAMED FOR SEXUAL HARASSMENT?

Workplace romances and sexually harassing behaviour have become commonplace in organizations. Workplace romances are mutually desired relationships involving physical attraction between two employees of the same workplace (Pierce, 1998; Pierce and Aguinis, 2003). It is believed that if harassment occurs between women and male colleagues, then that is because of the consent from both sides. If supervisors harass women, it is mainly because of their power position and if subordinates harass women, it is because of their male ego of being working under women.

Majority of the respondents, i.e. 55.0 percent blamed both male as well as female for sexual harassment, if the harassment is from male colleague. 26.5 percent blamed males and 18.5 percent blamed females only, if sexual harassment is by a male colleague. However, if sexual harassment is done by male superordinates, majority of the women blamed males

TABLE 4.21
To Whom Women Blamed for Sexual Harassment

Blame	*Sexual Harassment*		
	Colleagues	*Superordinates*	*Subordinates*
Female	37 18.5%	10 5%	2 1%
Male	53 26.5%	175 87.5%	188 94%
Both	110 55%	15 7.5%	10 5%
Total	200	200	200

only, i.e. 87.5 percent because of their power positions at workplace. Only 7.5 percent blamed both male and female and 5.0 percent blamed females only. When sexual harassment is done by a male subordinate, majority of the women blamed males, i.e. 94.0 percent. They were of the opinion that male subordinates could not see women working as their superordinates. Therefore, they indulge in sexually harassing behaviour. Whereas only 1.0 percent blamed females and 5.0 percent blamed both males and females.

MEASURES TO CHECK THE PROBLEM OF SEXUAL HARASSMENT

One of the objectives of the present study being exploring the main factors that affect women's decision to lodge a complaint; it becomes essential to know what measures working women suggest to check the problem of sexual harassment. Since the majority of respondents reported that they were sexual harassed at the workplace, they were asked to report the measures to check the problem of sexual harassment.

Majority of the respondents, i.e. 31.0 percent reported that stringent laws could check the problem. They wanted strictness at the level of implementation and justice. Further, they wanted women to be bold enough to come out openly and

TABLE 4.22
Measures to Check Sexual Harassment

Measures	*Frequency*	*Percent*
Stringent Law	46	23.0
Bold role of women	43	21.5
Socialization of men	11	5.5
Support of family and friends	38	19.0
Stringent law and bold role of women	62	31.0
Total	200	100.0

raise voice against their exploitation at the workplace. There were 23.0 percent respondents who favoured strict punishment for the perpetrators. There were 21.5 percent respondents who wanted women to become strong to fight their own battle. There were 19.0 percent of respondents who reported that many women did not get any support from their family and friends. They were discouraged by the family members to raise voice against authorities, as they never wanted them to be labeled. 11 respondents wanted men to be properly socialized. They blamed mindset of men for the existence of the problem of sexual harassment. All these explanations clearly indicate that women felt that weak personality of the women makes men more aggressive and exploitation of women at workplace continued in a characteristic manner.

CONCLUSION

The increase of women's share of employment since the mid-seventies resulted from a shift of women's labour from the unpaid household work and subsistence agricultural sector to the paid economy mostly in manufacturing and services in developing countries. Women workers have been in increased demand globally, because they can be hired for lower pay and under lower quality working conditions in comparison to men. The majority of women are still in irregular jobs with little training or promotion prospects and no or very limited job or social security.

Despite worldwide increase in women's paid employment in recent years, occupational segregation by sex continues to exist. Higher levels of occupational segregation are associated with poorer labour market conditions for women such as lower pay, lower status and more limited career opportunities, including higher chances of being subjected to sexual harassment. Occupational segregation by Women are more likely to be working in 'men's jobs' than the opposite and this again increases chances of sexual harassment of women.

A majority of countries worldwide have adopted some form of legislation at national level that covers sexual harassment. In most countries sexual harassment has been addressed by implication as an activity which is a violation of a statute covering a subject other than sexual harassment, such as human rights, non-discrimination, equal opportunity and treatment, unfair dismissal, contract law, tort law, or criminal law. Slowly but clearly, implicit protection of sexual harassment is giving way to explicit recognition and protection against acts of sexual harassment in many of these laws. This trend is occurring in countries in Asia and the Pacific as well as in other regions of the world.

In the present study it has been found that sexual harassment is quite prevalent at the workplace and is rising. The rise can mostly be attributed to underreporting. Majority of the illiterate women have no awareness about this problem and its redressal. Mostly educated women come forward to complain. For the women working in unorganized sector unwelcome remarks, verbal and non-verbal conduct of sexual nature is a part of their day-to-day life. As a result, they do not consider it as sexual harassment. Further, as asserted by the socio-cultural framework women's lower status in the larger society is reflected at the workplace structures and culture; consequently, male dominance continues to be the rule. Men are naturally reluctant to relinquish this superior position of privilege. Furthermore, men are socialized into roles of sexual assertion whereas women are socialized to be passive. These socio-cultural roles are played out at the workplace, and sexual harassment is the result. Sexual harassment reflects the larger society's differential distribution of power and status between the sexes. Additionally, it was also observed that perception of majority of the women in the study coincided with the definition given by the Supreme Court. They had awareness about the subject and propagated strong actions against the perpetrators but were themselves reluctant to take strong actions.

The main findings of the present chapter are as under:

- Majority of the respondents were sexually harassed by their superordinates.
- Majority of the respondents, i.e. between the age of 25-35 years faced more sexual harassment by their colleagues, superordinates and subordinates.
- Majority of the married respondents were sexually harassed by their colleagues, superordinates and subordinates. Whereas, single women faced more sexual harassment by their subordinates.
- Educated respondents faced more sexual harassment by their colleagues, superordinates and subordinates.
- Women working in middle level occupations faced more sexual harassment by their colleagues and subordinates. Whereas, women working in upper level occupations faced more sexual harassment by their superordinates.
- Majority of the respondents disagreed with the mild forms of sexual harassment, i.e. unwelcome remarks, verbal and non-verbal conduct of sexual nature and sexually visual material but agreed with the severe forms of the sexual harassment, i.e. unwelcome demands and physical contacts.
- Perception of the respondents of all age groups, marital status, caste, religion and occupations coincided with the Supreme Court's definition of sexual harassment.
- Majority of the respondents wanted to take some kind of active action against the perpetrator. But very few respondents when were sexually harassed complained against the perpetrator.

- Majority of the respondents blamed males only if sexual harassment is done by superordinates and subordinates. Both males and females were blamed when sexual harassment is done by a male colleague.
- Majority of the respondents wanted stringent laws and bold action by women to check the problem of sexual harassment.

5

Case Studies and Analysis

The significance of case study method is to get in depth knowledge about the problem of sexual harassment, which we cannot get in quantitative data. The concept of case study is frequently associated with qualitative research. Social Scientists, in particular, have made use of this qualitative research method to examine contemporary real-life situations and provide the basis for application of ideas and extension of methods. Robert K. Yin defines, 'the case study research method as an empirical inquiry that investigates a contemporary phenomenon within its real-life context; when the boundaries between phenomenon and context are not clearly evident; and in which multiple sources of evidence are used.' The present study attempts to focus on the following objectives in order to obtain the information on the problem of sexual harassment of women at workplace.

- To highlight the problem of sexual harassment of women at workplace.
- To find out how women cope up with this problem, i.e., the coping mechanisms used by women to deal with sexual harassment at workplace.

- To understand the types of action taken by the respondents to end their harassment.

To obtain information on the above said objectives, case study method has been used. Case studies are one of the most popular methods of conducting social science research. Despite the widespread use of case studies there is little consensus about what the term actually means. What is clear is that the definition of what constitutes a case study has changed over time and varies between social science disciplines and individual researchers. For some researchers case study research includes a single case, otherwise the research is regarded as comparative and not case study research. Other researchers consider that the number of cases is not an important issue. A central concept used in social science research is the idea of having cases as the building blocks for data collection and analysis. The main advantage of case study method is that it involves an in-depth study of each case. The most theoretical advantage of the case study is that it attempts to organize data around the unit of growth or group structure or individual life pattern. Another advantage of this method is that repeated visits to the case provide detailed information. It leads to a new insight and thus highlights the hidden aspect of one's life. Other advantage of the case study method includes its applicability to real life contemporary human situations and its public acceptability through written reports. In general, case studies make no claims to be representative. A major drawback of case study method is that it is not possible to generalize statistically from one or small number of cases. It is impossible to determine how far the findings of a study into one example of a social phenomenon can be applied to other examples. One way to overcome this problem is to choose a case or cases which are typical and contain certain cluster characteristics that are representative of other cases.

Case study research excels in bringing to us an understanding of a complex issue or object and can extend experience or add strength to what is already known through previous research. Case studies emphasize detailed contextual analysis of a limited number of events or conditions and their relationships. Case study method is an ideal methodology when a holistic, in-depth investigation is needed.

In the present study, 10 case studies have been included. The cases selected were interviewed on several occasions so that detailed information could be procured. Keeping in view, the objectives of the study in depth interviews and probing were relied upon to bring out their subterranean life circumstances. The cases have been presented in this chapter in a systematic manner, i.e. their background, causes of harassment, traits of the perpetrator, consequences of harassment on the victim at workplace, action taken by the victims, etc. To maintain secrecy, the first letter of their first names has been used. The cases that have lodged a formal complaint against the perpetrator have been included; further snowball technique has been used to collect the cases.

CASE–B

Ms. B is a 44 years old Hindu widow. She belongs to a Brahmin family. She is working as a peon in a Government office at Chandigarh.

Born in Amritsar, she has been brought up in a nuclear family. Her father is a small businessman. Her mother was illiterate housewife. Ms. B belongs to a lower middle class family. They are four sisters and two brothers and she is the youngest of all. Her all siblings are married and well settled.

Ms. B is a Matriculate from a Government school at Amritsar. She was an average student. However, she regularly took part in extra curricular activities and was good in sports. She was very extrovert and made friends easily. After completing her studies at the age of 18 years she took a temporary job in a Government office. She got this job on someone's recommendation.

When she was 20 years old, she got married in her own caste. Her husband was four years elder to her. It was an arranged marriage. Her husband was a Graduate and was in Government job with handsome salary. He belonged to joint family which was economically well-off. After marriage, she left her job. Unfortunately within two years of marriage, her husband expired due to heart attack. She did not have any issue from this marriage. After her husband's death, she was forced to go to her parents. She again started working because of the economic needs. She joined a private office on daily wages.

She remarried to a boy who was two years elder to her after a gap of two years. She met the boy while travelling in a bus and got involved with him. He belonged to an economically well-off Khatri family. Ms. B's parents openly accepted their marital alliance however, boy's family did not agree to this marriage, as she was a widow. Inspite of resistance of boy's parents they got married. Boy's parents did not accept them even after marriage. After that her husband's parents detached him from the family business, he started working in a shop. After one year of marriage, she was blessed with a daughter.

Her husband who was earlier a social drinker became an alcoholic due to economic difficulties and rejection by the family. His alcoholic behaviour became cause of marital conflict. On and off they had fights that often resulted in physical violence against her. During this period she gave birth to a son. They had very difficult time financially as her husband started spending the entire income on alcohol and they had no support from the kinsmen.

She developed animosity against her in-laws and decided to shift from Ludhiana to Chandigarh, as she wanted to wean away her husband from his parents. They started living in a rented house. In Chandigarh, her husband took a job in a shop. His salary was insufficient to meet their daily needs. To fulfil their requirements she started working as a sales-woman in a shop.

It was at her working place where she met a man. She developed friendship with him and found him very understanding and helpful. He was unmarried and younger to her. She started meeting him daily. He was in a government job. She started sharing all her family problems with him. He helped her in getting a permanent job of a peon in his own office. Her husband somehow got an inkling that she was going around with someone that increased the events of quarrels between them. Her husband asked her to terminate her relations with that man, to which she did not agree. There was lot of conflict and tension between them. After two years, her second husband also died due to alcoholism. After her husband's death, her boyfriend started visiting her. Both of them decided not to get married and continued their relationship. There was lot of pressure on the boy to get married by his parents. After taking her consent he got married to a girl of his parent's choice. However, they continued to work and meet at workplace after his marriage.

At her workplace, the number of male employees was more than the female employees. There was no discrimination between male and female employees regarding the work. She always had good relations with male as well as female employees in her work place. There were no complaints against her regarding her work and conduct. She was satisfied with her job as it was secured. The working hours were relaxed with lots of benefits. During her work she faced sexual harassment by one of her bosses, who was 64 years old. He was a widower with two sons who were married but living separately. Right from the beginning the behaviour of the Manager was not good with any of the female employees. He always misbehaved with them. He always used double meaning words like open the flap of file, giving an indirect reference of the under garments. Whenever he was standing in front of a female employee, he used to roll his tongue on his lips. Ms. B faced the same problem. She was 40 years old at that time. The boss's conduct was not acceptable to any of the female employees. But none could dare to speak against him.

Ms. B shared this problem with her male friend. He suggested her to give a written complaint against the Manager. But she did not agree to it. The Manager kept on misbehaving with her by using verbal obscene innuendoes. Ms. B started avoiding him, but did not take any action.

Ms. B continued to face harassment from her boss for one year. This one-year was not really comfortable for her. She had to face many psychological as well as physical problems. Due to tension, she could not sleep at night. She continued to ignore his waywardness till her son got injured in an accident and called her in the office. The boss received the call but misinformed her son that she was not present in the office. She came to know about her son's accident on reaching home in the evening. It really made her angry. Next day, in the office when she inquired from the Manager reasons for not conveying the correct message, he misbehaved with her. At this stage she decided to lodge a written complaint to higher authorities. Thereafter, the Manager was immediately transferred out of Chandigarh. Every one at the workplace appreciated her for her courage. She felt that her action played a very positive role in changing the working atmosphere of the office. She personally felt that any woman facing such problems at workplace should fight against the harasser.

CASE–K

Ms. K is a 49 years old married Hindu Khatri lady. She is working on an administrative post in University with handsome salary.

Born in a town named Khanna in Punjab, Ms. K comes from a well to do urban, educated, nuclear family. Her father retired as Superintendent of Police. Her mother is a housewife. She has one younger brother and sister. Her brother is also an Inspector in police and her sister is a Lecturer. She has cordial relations with her parents and siblings. She is very close to her mother. She shares each and everything with her mother.

The family shifted to Chandigarh on her father's transfer. She completed her schooling in a co-educational school and post-graduation in all girls' college from Chandigarh. She is also a diploma holder in Library Science and Office Management. Academically, she was a mediocre student. She used to participate actively in the co-curricular activities. She was very extrovert and made friends easily. Wherever she went, she used to fill the atmosphere with mirth and joy.

When Ms. K was doing her diploma in Library Science, she developed a close proximity with the librarian who was 10 years elder to her. He did not belong to her caste. She disclosed her feelings for this man to her mother. However, her mother did not agree to this relationship as there was age gap and the man belonged to different caste. Ms. K accepted her parent's decision and married to a man of her parent's choice. The boy was law graduate and working in a government office with handsome salary. He belonged to her caste and was only three years elder to her. After marriage, she shared her past with her husband who appreciated her honesty. They developed close and intimate relationship. Her husband has three brothers and all the brothers are landlords. She has very good and friendly relation with her in-laws.

After completing her studies, she got a job in the University through her father's recommendation and till date she is continuing with the job and has risen to higher ranks. Ms. K always wanted to be independent. She worked for two years before marriage. After marriage also, she continued to work and her husband and in-laws did not object to her working. She has grown up children. Her daughter is doing Ph.D. in the U.S. and is going to get married in near future. Her son is doing Engineering at Chandigarh. She has very friendly relations with her daughter and son. Both of them share each and everything with her.

She always liked her work and did it with full enjoyment. She is fond of her job and finds it quite comfortable. Her work timings are from 9.00 a.m. to 5.00 p.m. At her work place the female–male ratio is almost equal. She has friendly and cordial relations with all colleagues. There is no discrimination between male and female employees regarding the work. She is very much devoted to her work. There have never been any complaints against her. Ms. K had healthy relations with her subordinates and superordinates at workplace.

However, she did experience sexual harassment at her work place. Her immediate senior, who was 50 years old married man with grown up children tried to harass her. He always used to flirt with the female employees. He was very abusive and would start his sentence by calling names and Ms. K was a kind of person who would not tolerate such behaviour. She always resented his behaviour. He would come and sit where female employees were sitting and would pass some obnoxious remarks. His remarks had all the undertones of sexual misdemeanor. He always indulged in frivolous talks and called ladies 'sexy, gorgeous, stunning, Cleopatra, lightening', etc. He habitually passed such base remarks in front of other male employees also and his attitude always made female employees feel embarrassed. No one however, took any action against him and treated him as mentally sick. Most of them ignored his comments.

Ms. K was also facing the same problem. But as a self-respecting lady, she always warned him not to misbehave with her. Her senior could not digest her resentment and felt that she was humiliating him. No one had dared to raise any objection about his misbehaviour. He thought that he was all in all and his subordinates must dance to his tunes without saying a word. He had a notion that it was his right to take liberties with the ladies. Ms. K did not respond to his whims and warned him of the dire consequences in case he continued with the misbehaviour. In spite of warnings by Ms. K, her boss continued with his abusive and sexually offensive behaviour. Ms. K did not take any action against him because she was not coming to office on time. She knew that he would disciplinary action against her. Therefore she would just warn him not to take liberties with her but never informed the higher authorities.

One day, Ms. K reached her office half and hour late and she was asked to submit half-day leave. At this, Ms. K. protested and there was an exchange of hot words between them. Matter was settled with her colleagues asking her to submit an application. After this episode, her harassment increased manifold and he started passing obscene remarks with sexual connotations directly towards her. She got very much frustrated with her boss's behaviour. But she kept on ignoring his behaviour. Right from the beginning, Ms. K was sharing her problem with her husband. He suggested her to lodge a complaint against the boss to higher authorities. But Ms. K did not do so. She thought things will settle down with time. But it did not happen.

Ms. K was not allowing her boss to take liberties with her. He started harassing her all the more. He even spoiled her annual career report. He wrote hasty remarks about her. That made her furious. She decided to settle the scores with him. Other female colleagues decided to join her in filing the complaint but at the last moment they backed out. But Ms. K did not lose heart. Her husband gave her support at this crucial time and she gave written complaint against the boss to higher authorities. When her boss came to know about the complaint, he started threatening her. He warned her of dire consequences. But Ms. K did not succumb to his pressures as she had full support of her family.

After filing the complaint authorities held an enquiry. Ms. K fought for 3 months to get justice and this period was really full of tension for her. She faced embarrassment, anxiety, lowered self-esteem as well as psychological disorders. At the time when enquiry was going on her boss was not placed under suspension. They continued to work in the same workplace. He continued to stare at her at work place. He made things miserable for her. It was a very traumatic period of her life. To pressurize her, boss started roaming around her home with his young son and would stare at her. Things became from bad to worse.

She approached the office union and asked for favours. Consequently her boss was transferred to a different branch. It lessened her trauma to some extent. He continued to threaten her by sending messages through common sources that he would commit suicide and blame her.

After enquiry, the higher authorities found the boss guilty and recommended termination of his service. She requested the authorities for her own transfer. She did not want his services to be terminated. Her only purpose was to highlight the existence of sexual harassment at work place and set an example for victims. He was demoted and continued to work in the same place.

Ms. K feels that her complaint had a positive effect on other female employees at the work place. Even the other male colleagues started behaving respectfully with female employees. Her female colleagues expressed their gratitude towards her. She felt very honoured. She feels that she has done a good job for women's welfare. She was transferred to some other department where she enjoys respect of all her colleagues.

CASE–J

Ms. J is a 25 years old Graduate. She belongs to a Sikh nuclear family. She is a freelancer who writes for a Human Rights Magazine. She highlights the social issues existing in the society. Ms. J belongs to Chandigarh. Her parents are well educated. Her father is a Postgraduate and mother is a Graduate. Her father used to work in a private company. Now, he has retired from the service. Her mother is a housewife. She belongs to an upper middle class family with a sound financial background. Ms. J has one brother who after completing his M.B.A. has gone to Australia and is now well settled there.

Ms. J completed her entire education at Chandigarh. She is a Graduate and has also done Diploma in French and a course from Airhostess academy. She did her schooling from a co-educational school. She was an extrovert and was very friendly with her male class fellows. She was mediocre at studies. She always participated actively in cultural activities. After graduating at the age of 20 years, she got trained as an Airhostess and started working for an Airline company. It was when her friend was called for an interview at Bangalore for job of an Airhostess in Jet Airways, she accompanied her and appeared for the interview. She got selected.

Her parents were very open-minded. They provided her all the opportunities in her life and always respected her decision. They allowed her to join the Airlines. She knew that it was a difficult job but she accepted this challenge confidently and moved on. She stayed in Bangalore for six months and worked with Jet Airways. Having gained experience she made quick change over. She got selected for a more prestigious British Airways in London at a handsome salary and worked there for 8 months. Then, she opted to work in Emirates Airways in Dubai for a year. Ms. J holds that in these two years and two months, she learnt a lot. When Ms. J was working in Emirates Airways her physical health started deteriorating. Her doctor suggested that she was facing health problems because of her profession. She started remaining ill most of the time. Her parents asked her to leave the job. Thus due to ill health she left the job of airhostess during the span of two years. She did not face any kind of sexual harassment from her male superordinates, colleagues, subordinates and customers during this period.

Ms. J came back to Chandigarh and joined her parents for the sake of her health. She decided to work in Chandigarh. She gave an Interview in Airhostess Academy and got selected as an instructor. She started working as a Front Office Executive and a trainer too. Her income was Rs. 15000 per month, which was quite meager, as she has been earning in lakhs earlier. At her work place, there were two males and six females. One male was senior officer and one was subordinate to her. Her work timings were from 10.00 a.m. to 5.00 p.m. There were no shift duties and travelling. Ms. J found this job very interesting, as she has to interact with new people everyday.

Ms. J worked in the Airhostess Academy for a period of ten months and due to her hard work and dedication she was confirmed after a period of six months with an enhanced salary. Her senior officer who was 50 years old joined the academy after seven months of her joining. He was not a man of good character. Soon, he started making advances towards her. He started making passes at her, showering compliments and praises on her to win over her, like "you are very beautiful" and "God has made you in free time." Initially Ms. J ignored his behaviour and later snubbed him that they were not there to exchange compliments. To do work with dedication was her sole motive. He further tried to allure her by telling her repeatedly that he was going through a bitter matrimonial experience with his wife and he needed somebody to share his feelings. When Ms. J did not respond to his advances, his misbehaviour continued for two to three months. He used every tactic to impress her but she did not fall into his trap. He resorted to pressure tactics by sending complaints against her to the Head Office regarding her work and conduct viz. she was a habitual late comer and an inefficient executive. One day, he crossed all the limits by alleging that she had taken the money collected from students as fine for violation of various rules.

The senior officer started insulting her on pity matters and did not lose any opportunity to demean her. He looked for the occasion to mentally harass her. Ms. J faced the problem of sexual harassment for 3 months and during this period due to tension, her physical health started deteriorating. In the beginning, she did not share her problems with her parents because she was of the view that she could handle her official problems on her own. However, when things became difficult for her and she was not able to cope with the stress in the job, she disclosed the problem to her parents. Soon after knowing the problem her parents compelled her to leave the job. Further, for her job was not a necessity. Her parents did not allow her to inform the higher authorities as they were of the opinion that the superordinate would manipulate the matter according to his convenience. Ms. J wanted to fight for justice. After convincing her parents, she lodged a formal complaint in the labour court as her superordinate withheld her salary of two months. At the time of recording of this case study, she was fighting for justice. She had not received any relief.

Ms. J is of the view that only males are responsible for the existence of the problem of sexual harassment in the society. When she worked in odd hours (as an airhostess), she did not face any sexual harassment from any of her colleagues, superordinates or subordinates. But when she was working in normal hours, she had to face sexual harassment on the hands of her super ordinate. She thinks, it depends only on the socialization of men that how they perceive women as sex objects. Ms. J holds that a woman must fight against the problem of sexual harassment. Culprit should be brought to books. Otherwise such men would continue to harass women.

CASE–E

Ms. E is 28 years old Sikh married woman. At present she is working as Deputy Director in a Government Office on contractual basis. Born in Chandigarh, Ms. E was brought up in a nuclear family. Her father was in a Government job but could not complete his services and left his job on the health grounds. Her mother is a housewife. She had to face economic hardships in the childhood. Ms. E has two sisters and one brother and she is the youngest of them all. Her brother is working in a private company and her sister-in-law is a housewife. Both her sisters are happily married and are well settled. She has very friendly relations with her sisters. Hers is a close-knit family.

Ms. E completed her schooling from a Government school at Chandigarh. She studied in a co-educational school. She was a friendly child. In studies, she was a mediocre and shy student, as a result not very participative in extra-curricular activities. After her schooling, she completed a course in the Nursing and started working because of the economic need of the family. She worked as Nurse in a private organization on meager salary. However, she continued with her education. She appeared as a private candidate for Graduation and Post-graduation. After improving her qualification, she changed her job. In spite of different difficulties, she worked hard to improve her qualification. She completed her Ph.D. after marriage to get better job opportunities. Before taking up the present job she worked for eleven years in three different non-government organizations, mostly in research projects.

She got married at the age of 24 years with a Hindu Jat boy of her choice with the consent of her parents. Her husband is a MBA and 5 years elder to her. He was working with her in an organization and there they developed intimacy with each other. After working together for one and a half year, they got married. It was an inter-caste marriage. She was married in a joint family. Her father-in-law was in the Army and is since retired. Her mother-in-law is a housewife. Ms. E's husband is the only son of his parents. Her two sister-in-laws are married and are well settled. After one year of marriage, she gave birth to twin daughters. She is in a very good terms with her in-laws. She continued to work even after marriage.

Ms. E started working at an early age. She worked in different private organizations. She worked at odd hours, travelled with male colleagues but developed cordial relations with them. It was in one of the organizations, where she worked as a Social Scientist. She faced the problem of sexual harassment. She had very good relations with her male as well as female colleagues at the workplace. Male and female employees were treated equally at her workplace. She always liked her work and did it with full sincerity. Her superordinates were happy with her performance. There had never been any complaints against Ms. E as she was very efficient in her work.

She had been working in this private organization for the last three years, when a new male colleague who was about 30 years old joined as a Computer Typist in the office. He always used to come drunk to the office. In spite of his addiction, he was quite efficient. The superordinates ignored his drinking habit.

Due to requirement of the job, Ms. E had to interact with this computer typist on regular basis. Initially, she did not face any problem. But gradually she noticed that he started passing vulgar remarks in front of her. She ignored his behaviour. He started passing unwelcome personal remarks having sexual connotations about her looks, dress and body contours, etc. He realized that she did not react. She continued to ignore his remarks till she felt that they were not personalized. It became a routine affair, she would meet him for job purposes and he would comment on her looks. This disturbed her peace of mind. She could not concentrate on her work. She started avoiding him. She stopped going to him. Her work started suffering. She felt miserable. She did not think of talking to her superiors. She did not even share the matter with her fiancée, because she thought that her fiancées ill temperament would make the matter worse. Ms. E faced harassment for a month and this period was really traumatic for her. She noticed that computer typist did not misbehave with other female employees. He used to target her at every available opportunity. As time passed by, things became quite apparent to everyone at workplace. Other colleagues in the Office started talking about the matter. Ms. E's situation became awkward. She felt very embarrassed, helpless and vulnerable. She even could not sleep at nights. All the employees were aware of the fact that this computer typist was targeting Ms. E But they did not share anything with Ms. E.

When things became unbearable, Ms. E decided to talk to one of her female colleagues. Her colleague suggested her to complain against him to the higher authority. Ms. E was not sure how her superordinates would react. Further, she never wanted to be in limelight for wrong reasons as such she did complain immediately. She started thinking about making a formal complaint as her perpetrator continue with his waywardness. In the meantime, her female colleague complained to her immediate boss who was a lady officer. The lady officer was highly disturbed about the whole episode and decided to take immediate action. The Computer typist was sacked on the allegations of inefficient work, coming to office in the drunken state and misbehaving with a female colleague. When Ms. E came to know about his dismissal, it was a big relief for her. Her name did not figure directly in the whole episode.

Ms. E who has worked with male coworkers mentioned that staring and passing comments about female colleagues is a major pass time among males in most of the work organizations. She reported that large number of women ignore it; as a result problem of sexual harassment goes unnoticed in the workplace. It is brought to notice only when it takes ugly turn or results in physical assault. She argued that women keep silent to avoid being stigmatized because women who make complaints face insecurity with regard to job, she considered herself lucky as she got justice by not making tireless efforts.

CASE–T

Ms. T is a 49 years old married Sikh lady. At present she is working as Assistant Sub Inspector in Chandigarh Police and started her career as a Constable in Police. She is serving the Chandigarh Police with high dedication and honesty for the last 28 years. Her monthly income is approximately Rs. 20,000.

She was born in Chandigarh. She is from an economically well-off nuclear family. Both her parents are well educated. Her father served in the Army. Her mother is a housewife. She has a younger sister as the only sibling, who is married and is a Lecturer. Her parents being educated themselves were in favour of providing good education to their daughters. Both the sisters, got education according to their own interests. Her father believed in freedom of thought. He was rather idealistic, believer in the good and right things, so none of the daughters were ever forced to choose a particular stream of education. They got complete freedom to select their career.

Ms. T was an average all round student. She did her schooling from Chandigarh. Her father was in Army and kept on getting postings at different places. Her mother stayed with them at Chandigarh. She studied in a co-educational school. She was very extrovert. She had very open relations with her parents and sister. She shared all her problems with her family members. After completing graduation, she joined police force; which is considered to be a male dominated occupation.

At the age of 25 years, she married the boy of her own choice. Her parents, without any objection, gave their consent. She met her husband through a common friend and developed intimacy with him. Her husband is a Graduate in Arts and a Businessman. He earns approximately Rs. 40,000 per month. She has only one daughter, who is doing M.B.B.S.

Ms. T, inspired by her father, always wanted to serve her country. So, she adopted police force. She had to work in shift duties. Travelling was very rare in her work. She always had very good and cordial relations with the males at her workplace. She was very happy with her profession. Being in a male dominated occupation, the number of male superordinates, colleagues and subordinates was high at her workplace. During her Police life, she did face many odd situations at times. Many a times, criminals threatened her whom she caught on different cases. It was a tough job but she continued to work with great zeal and spirit.

She faced sexual harassment at the hands of male superordinate when she faced an official enquiry. The enquiry was instituted on a complaint made by a criminal against her. The complainant had been charged with eve teasing by Ms. T. He lodged complaint against Ms T to malaise his image in the Human Rights Commission. The Police Department appointed a senior 52 year old, Police Inspector as an enquiring officer. The Inspector would call her late in the evening to join the enquiry. She showed her inability to join the enquiry in the late hours. When she repeatedly refused to abide by his orders, he called her at 5:00 p.m. at Police Headquarters. She reached at Police Headquarters at 4.55 p.m. but the Inspector was not there. After waiting for about one and half hours, she returned home. Same day at about 8.00 p.m. she received a call from the Inspector again to report at his house for the enquiry. She again showed her inability to join enquiry at odd hours.

Next day, when she was performing her duties in a Hotel, the Inspector came to her, started showering of abuses upon her. He used abusive, derogatory language against her with an intention to insult her in presence of a number of persons. To quote his words: "TU MAINU FUDU BANA RAHI HAIN, HUN MAIN TAINU FUDU BANA KE DASANGA. TO DO KAURI DI AURAT APNE AAP NU KI SAMAJH DI HAIN, MAIN TAINU DASANGA KE MARD KI HUNDA HAI." It was very embarrassing moment for Ms. T. Her other colleagues who were witness to whole episode mentioned the bad reputation of Police Inspector. She came to know that he was a corrupt police official and had faced CBI enquiry in that regard. Her colleagues warned her of dire consequences. They mentioned that she had not done right to get into conflicting situation with him. He was known as quite an arrogant and high-headed official.

She reported the incident to her husband and both of them decided to take some action against the erring Inspector. She complained to the higher official but no action was taken against the Inspector. As, she was working in male dominated occupation, no male colleague supported her for her action. Rather, she herself was blamed. When no action was taken by the higher officials, she brought the issue to public consciousness through media. It was then; the matter was taken up by various Human Rights Organizations and the social workers. The media also played a vital role in exposing the exclusive case of sexual harassment and insult of a woman, particularly, who herself was the lady A.S.I. In spite of the fact that Police Department runs Crime against Women Cell, women in their own department are harassed a lot.

Sexual harassment made Ms. T felt very irritable; her emotional reactions included anger, fear, depression, anxiety, lowered self-esteem, feelings of humiliations, vulnerability, etc. In spite of all this, she continued to enjoy the support of her husband. He showed complete confidence and faith in her. At the time of recording of this case history Ms. T did not receive any justice. She is still suffering from mental torture, agony and embarrassment. Her superordinates are upset with her for bringing bad name to Police Force. Her female colleagues avoid her company. Her subordinates make fun of her. She has become a topic of discussion at her workplace. This episode has jeopardized her career. She has dared to challenge the male ego in male dominating occupation. The retaliation against her action has been so severe that hardly any women in the Police force would think of bringing the culprit to books. She prays that the accused be punished in the interest of justice. She is of the opinion that her fight against sexual harassment will definitely prove beneficial to other working females and it will teach men to respect women.

CASE–S

Ms. S is a 40 years old married Hindu lady. She is Aggarwal by caste. She is working as a Teacher in a Private School in Chandigarh. Her monthly salary is approximately Rs. 15,000.

Born in Patiala, she was brought up in an economically well-off nuclear family. Her father is a Doctor and her mother is a housewife. Her mother is educated upto Senior Secondary. She has one brother and one sister, both are elder to her. Her brother is a Doctor. Her sister-in-law is a Post-graduate and is a housewife. Her sister is a Lecturer. She has been brought up in a very open atmosphere by her parents.

Her parents never imposed any restrictions on her. She describes her parents as very gentle and kind hearted. She completed her schooling and Post-graduation from Patiala. She has also done M.Ed. She studied in a co-educational college. She was a brilliant student. She used to actively participate in co-curricular activities. She is a very extrovert and make friend easily.

After completing studies, she became teacher as she was very fond of children. She always wanted to be independent. She taught in a private school at Patiala for 2 years. She was married off at the age of 25 by her parents. Her husband is 5 years elder to her and belonged to same caste. He was a Law Graduate and was working as a Lawyer in Chandigarh. After marriage, she settled in Chandigarh.

She got married in a highly educated family. Her father-in-law is a retired senior judge. Her mother-in-law is a Graduate and she is a housewife. Ms. S's husband has two brothers. One brother is settled in the U.S. and one brother is a Class-I official. Her sister-in-law is a Law Graduate and is a housewife.

After one year of her marriage, she was blessed with a son. She got busy in the up bringing of her son. She gave birth to her second son after the gap of one year. She could not think of joining any job. She became busy with her family and children. When both of her sons started going to school, she was left alone at home and she used to feel very lonely. She planned to work again at the age of 31 years. She got an English teacher's job in a private school at Chandigarh through her husband's recommendations.

She found her job very interesting and enjoyable. She had relaxed working hours, i.e. 8.00 a.m. to 2.00 p.m. She would take care of her children and job in a best possible manner. In her workplace, she had very cordial and friendly relations with her male as well as female colleagues. She did not face any discrimination at her work place. The school atmosphere was very good. She never faced any problem in the school. After 5 years, the Principal got transferred and the new male Principal joined who was 55 years old married man with two children.

The new Principal did not show any respect to female teachers. He used to misbehave with all the female teachers in the school. He had the habit of winking at the female teachers. He used to feign blinking or roll his tongue on his lips in front of female employees. He used to call up female teachers to his office on one excuse or other. Almost all female teachers were upset with his behaviour but no one could dare to protest. She felt harassed for the first time when the Principal looked at her with lewd and exploring way in front of other staff members. It really made her embarrassed. And day-by-day, the harassment of the Principal increased. Ms. S discussed this problem with her husband. Her husband suggested her to lodge a complaint against the Principal with higher authorities. But she did not gather courage to complain against him. She thought, things would get settled with time. She continued to go through trauma of harassment.

The Principal continued with his waywardness. He used to call her to his office on and off and always used to talk irrelevant things. She was getting mentally disturbed. She tried to warn him but he persisted with his behaviour. One day, the Principal caught hold of her hand. She felt highly disturbed and discussed the matter with a senior male staff member who tried to intervene in the matter. But the Principal made excuses and continued with his behaviour. He again misbehaved with her. She again made an oral complaint to the senior staff member, who warned the principal again but in vain. After these complaints, the Principal's behaviour became all the more annoying and harassing. He started torturing her mentally. He used to insult her in the assembly, in the staff room, in front of the other teachers for no reason. Ms. S felt miserable and stressed. She discussed the matter again with her husband. After lot of persuasion she decided to give a written complaint to the Managing Committee of the school.

The Principal using his power reconstituted the Managing Committee of the school and included his favourite in it as members; she was forced by the Chairperson of the Managing Committee to take her complaint back failing which she was threatened by him of dire consequences. She did not take the complaint back. As a result, she was suspended from her service on the basis of false allegations like negligence of duties and creating false propaganda against authorities. She stayed at home for two months. This was a period of great distress and agony for her. She continued to fight her battle against injustice because all the time she had support of her husband. In the mean time, her husband being lawyer asked her to take legal action. She filed a case in the Court against her dismissal. Three of her female colleagues who were also being harassed by the Principal joined her and gave their statements against him in the High Court. It was out of vengeance that Principal has suspended her. The Court ordered the management for her reinstatement. She was reinstated but was not given any work. She was not given teaching work because management wanted to teach her a lesson. For the last two years, she has been going to school but does not teach. The Principal does not cross his limits with her. The Principal however, still misbehaves with other female employees of the school. She has filed another case against the authorities. At the time of recording of this case study, she did not receive any justice. Ms. S feels, her battle for justice may go in vain; because by the time she will get justice the Principal might get retired.

There was no Sexual Harassment Cell in the school. She faced physical as well as emotional harassment. Her physical ailments included nausea, headache, loss of appetite, inability to sleep and emotional trauma included anger, depression, anxiety and a feeling of helplessness. But her husband and family gave her full support and encouraged her to fight against the Principal.

When Ms. S made a formal complaint, other female employees also felt happy. They thought that after the complaint, the Principal would not misbehave with other female employees. But it did not happen. The Principal kept on misbehaving with other female employees except Ms. S.

Ms. S feels, "the women who are being sexually harassed at workplace, should collectively come forward to eradicate this problem from the society."

CASE–M

Ms. M is a 21 years old married Hindu lady. She has done Bachelors in Computer Application. At present, she is working as a Call Support Associate in a Call Center and is earning approximately Rs. 12,000 per month. Her husband is M.B.A and works in the same Call Center. Born in Chandigarh, Ms. M was brought up in a Rajput joint family. Her father is a Bank Manager and her mother looks after the household activities. Her father is a Post-graduate in Arts and her mother is a Matriculate. She has one elder brother, who is an Engineer. She has very friendly relations with her parents and other family members. She is from an economically well off family.

She completed her schooling from Chandigarh. She studied in a co-educational school. Academically, she was a brilliant student. She also actively participated in Sports, Quiz and Cultural activities. She was very extrovert and made friends easily. When Ms. M was 18 years old, she developed intimate relations with a boy who was 6 years elder to her and belonged to Jat family. He was their family friend's son. After 2 years of courtship, Ms. M informed her parents about her affair. In spite of the fact the families were known to each other, they refused to accept the relationship, as her husband was not economically independent. He was without any job.

After lot of persuasion her parents accepted their relationship. However, her husband's parents did not accept their relationship because of the caste factor. Despite their opposition Ms. M decided to get married. Her father-in-law is in Government Service. Her mother-in-law is a housewife. Her husband is the only son of his parents. Her in-laws did not accept her even after marriage. So, the newly married couple set-up their own home. Just after marriage, she and her husband started looking for a job.

They got job in a call center at fixed salary of Rs. 12,000 per month through an advertisement. Her husband also joined the job in the same Call Center on an identical salary. She found the job attractive because she was getting good salary and moreover, there were only young people at her workplace. She had to work at night also. Her working hours were from 9.00 p.m. to 4.00 a.m. and from 4.00 a.m. to 10.00 a.m. In the Call Center, there were five females and twenty males. She had cordial relations with colleagues and subordinates at the Call Center. However, the boss at the Call Center behaved differently towards female staff. He would always come drunk to the office. She realized that her boss was not a person of good character. The employees did not like her boss because; he always misbehaved with the females at the workplace.

Her boss was 45 years old, married man and had two children, a daughter and a son. After two days of joining the job, the boss also started misbehaving with her on the occasions by touching and caucusing exposed parts. Female employee resisted but did not say anything as most of them were in dire need of money. He held Ms. M's hands while talking, which made her very uncomfortable. She did not know how to react to her boss's advances. He misbehaved with all the female employees. He started doing the same to Ms. M. She started avoiding her boss but could not take any strong step against him, because she was also under financial constrain. She informed her husband, who told her to maintain distance from him or avoid him as much as possible. He assured her that they would leave the job as soon as they get a new opportunity.

Within a month's time, Ms. M got new job in another Call Center. They informed the boss and asked to clear their dues.

The boss refused to give their salaries. On their repeated requests, the boss did not release their wages. Ms. M and her husband decided to lodge a formal complaint against the boss. The other employees declined to support them. On the other hand, they informed the boss. When the boss came to know that Ms. M was going to lodge a complaint against him, he called her up. He requested her to settle the matter, as he did not want bad name for his center. He asked her to take her salary and not to complain to Police. She accepted his proposal and went to his office along with her husband. On reaching Office, he told her to come to his cabin alone. When she went inside his cabin, he offered half the salary. Ms. M refused to take the half salary. He started laughing at her. He agreed to give her full salary provided she spent night with him. She refused to his proposal. He got annoyed and called her woman of loose morale. He tried to molest her. Ms. M raised an alarm. Her husband immediately entered the cabin and thrashed the boss. He succeeded in saving her wife and they both went straight to the police station and wanted to lodge a formal complaint of sexual harassment against her boss. But in the police station, they were again harassed. The police did not lodge their complaint. Ms. M took the help of media and brought the issue in the knowledge of everyone. She lodged a formal complaint in the Labour Court for the release of her salary.

Ms. M had to go through many problems in her job. She was working under a fear and threat of sexual harassment every day. At every point of time, she felt insecure. Even after lodging complaint, she had to face social disgrace. Every third person started discussing about her problem which used to upset her. It was only because of the support of her husband, that she could lodge a complaint against the boss. Her husband encouraged her on every moment. Without her husband's support, it was not possible for her to take such an action.

She feels that every woman who is being harassed at workplace should come forward and teach the culprit a lesson. In the long-run, it will help other females at workplace. She feels, this problem exists in the society because of the under reporting of the problem. At the time of recording of this case study, she was fighting a legal battle against the culprit. She is working in another Call Center along with her husband. She feels that all men are not bad. There are some bad elements in the private organizations that can go to any extent to serve their purpose. She argues that women do not complain because of lack of support system, further many women work on lower wages. This weakness is known to their perpetrators and they exploit these women economically and sexually.

CASE–C

Ms. C is a 33 years old widow Hindu lady. She belongs to Scheduled caste. She is working for an NGO as peer educator. Her job is to create awareness about HIV/AIDS in the slums at Chandigarh. Her monthly income is Rs. 1500. Different projects are being run by the Government of India in city and adjoining areas with regard to AIDS awareness. Sex workers, intravenous drug users, migrant workers live in slum areas. In order to create awareness among them, different organizations assign job to people living in that area only to create awareness.

Ms. C was born in a village near Chandigarh. She was brought up in a nuclear family. She belongs to an illiterate family. Her father is working as a Peon in a private office. Her mother was a housewife and died 6 years ago due to Cancer. Ms. C has eight brothers and sisters. Her all siblings are illiterate. Ms. C spent her whole childhood in poverty and misery. They had hand to mouth existence.

Ms. C got married when she was 13 years old. The boy was also of the same caste. Her husband was a Matriculate and was working as a Mechanic. He was the only child of his parents. His parents are staying in village. Ms. C and her husband got settled in slum Chandigarh.

After three years of her marriage, she gave birth to a son and after 3 years to a daughter. At present, her son is 17 years old and is studying in 7th standard in the night school. Besides this, he works as a painter and is earning Rs. 1600 per month. Her daughter is 13 years old and is studying in 4th standard in the Government school in the slum, where she is staying. She was in good terms with her husband. Unfortunately, her husband died in an accident after 14 years of marriage. It was only after her husband's death that she started working as a maid outside home. There was no support from her family of orientation, who themselves were living in poverty.

She started working as a maid servant in different houses. She worked very hard as she had to feed her children. She did this job for two years. In the first year of her job, she was happy with her work. She was not facing any kind of problem at her workplace. But after one year, she faced sexual harassment. In one of the houses where she was working, male head of the family tried to sexually molest her. His wife was working and he sat idle at the home for the whole day. He used to pass sexually explicit remarks at her, like, she was sexy, young, she could get many men, etc. Initially, Ms. C ignored it. But he kept on harassing her by passing sexual remarks. She could not share her problem with anybody and also did not complain to his wife because of her economic compulsions, as she did not want to leave the job.

One day, she was asked to come in the afternoon for her chores, as they were expecting guests in the evening. When she reached, there was no work for her to do. The perpetrator caught hold of her and tried to rape her. She shouted for help. She could manage to run. However, he threatened her not to tell anybody; otherwise it would not be good for her and her family. He threatened her that he knew many Police Officials and he would blame her of theft. He gave her money and told her not to come to his house again. She got scared and left the house and did not talk about it to anyone. For few days she did not go to work. In the meantime she talked to her neighbour who was working as a sweeper in a private hospital. He helped her in getting job of a sweeper on daily wages.

She started working as a sweeper in a hospital. While working in the hospital, she realized that her male coworkers used to pass lewd remarks at her. She continued to ignore them as she was in dire need of work. She became friendly with one of the female sweeper. She talked to her about the annoying behaviour of the male sweepers. This lady asked Ms. C not to annoy them rather pleases them. She told Ms. C that in order to survive in the man's world, she has to obey men.

She asked Ms. C to provide sexual favours to those men otherwise they would not allow her to work in the hospital. Left with no alternative, Ms. C joined her friend. She developed physical intimacy with those men. These men provided her with gifts and money. Life became very easy for Ms. C. She started providing sexual favours to other men in exchange of money.

To the outside world, she was working as a sweeper in the private hospital, but actually she became full-fledged sex worker. She was able to provide all the facilities to her children. Her physical status also improved. She developed contacts with many affluent people. It was in this context she was able to get job as peer group educator with one of the NGO. She creates awareness about AIDS among sex workers and the precautions to be taken for protection.

She holds that she had faced a very miserable life and blames the society and her circumstances responsible for her present condition. Ms. C is of the opinion that it is very difficult for single woman to survive in this male dominating society. When she resisted other men's sexual advances, she was harassed and humiliated. The moment she agreed to their ways, she had a comfortable living. She feels that she became sex worker because women in society are viewed only as sex objects. They do not have any identity of their own. She, however, does not want her children to fall astray. For her, sexual harassment exists because of Gender Inequality. Unless and until women are given respect and equality, this problem cannot be checked.

CASE–P

Ms. P is 45 years old Hindu Schedule Caste widow, who works as maid servant in different homes. Her monthly income is Rs. 2000 and lives in a slum at Chandigarh. Born in a Village near Sirsa, she comes from a joint family. Her father was a daily wager and mother was a maid servant. They are six brothers and sisters. One of her brothers and a sister are elder to her and one brother and two sisters are younger to her. She belongs to poor illiterate family. She never went to school. She started helping her mother in her work since childhood.

Ms. P was 14 years old, when she was married to an illiterate boy of 18 years who was working on daily wages. He was living in a slum at Chandigarh. Her husband's parents were not living with them. They were three brothers. His parents and his brothers were living in a village in U.P. Her husband was earning Rs. 1500 per month. Ms. P has three children, two sons and a daughter after marriage. She continued to work as a maid servant. She was earning Rs. 1000 per month.

After six years of her marriage, her husband died due to alcoholism. There was no support from the family. After death of her husband, she continued her job. She started sending her children in a Government school in the slum. She started working hard. She did not find her work comfortable, because after her husband's death, male members of the families were harassing her, where she worked. In one incident, she was sexually harassed by a male member of the household, who was 35 years old. He used to pass sexually explicit remarks at her like, "you are very sexy, you are young, you don't earn much in this job; why don't you try some other profession." But Ms. P did not respond and did not even complain to his wife. She continued in her job due to economic compulsion. This male member tried to molest her physically but she succeeded in escaping herself. She felt very miserable, stressed, helpless, vulnerable, depressed as well as humiliated. So, she decided to take some legal action against the perpetrator. She approached a women's organization but in vain. She used to visit women's organization in routine for the enquiry but the perpetrator never gave his attendance. She could not get justice. The perpetrator got the case dismissed by using his power. She left that job and started working somewhere else.

Even the growing adolescent children started harassing her. Once, she was washing utensils in a house and a male adolescent of the family was alone at home. He showed Ms. P a porn magazine. On this, she slapped the boy and complained to his parents. The boy's parents did not accept her side of the story and forced her to quit the job. She is working as a maid servant for last 31 years. She had faced sexual harassment from very young and middle aged men at her workplace. She feels that rich men do not respect poor working women. They feel that women who come to work outside their homes do not have any dignity. Further, poor illiterate women do not know where to complain? Further, if she complains, there is no one to provide justice. "It is a rich man world." In order to safeguard her interest, she prefers to work in those households where women are not working. She avoids taking her daughter to her workplace. She mentions that most of the poor women are not as lucky as her and they are exploited by their paymasters. Government can check exploitation of women in formal setting but it is very difficult to arrest men who exploit poor women at their own houses. They try to exploit them as they have no fear and have full protection.

CASE–V

Ms. V is 44 years old married woman. She belongs to a Hindu middle class family. She is a Khatri by caste. At present, she is working as a Deputy Manager in a Public Sector Bank. Born in a small town, Hamirpur, Ms. V was brought up in a nuclear family. Her father is a Graduate and has since retired from a Government service. Her mother is a housewife. Ms. V has only one brother, who is elder to her. Her brother and sister-in-law are well educated and are working in Government offices. She has friendly relations with her family members. She always used to share her problem with her parents.

Ms. V. completed her schooling and college in Government institutes at Hamirpur. She studied in all girls' school. She has always been a topper and was also very participative in extra curricular activities. She was very popular with her teachers. After her Graduation, she started preparing the entrance test for the job in Banks. At the age of 24 years, she got through the exam and started working as a clerk in a Public Sector Bank. She got married at the age of 30 years.

Her husband is one year younger to her and belonged to her caste. He is a Graduate and works in a Government office in Chandigarh. On special requests to the authorities she got herself transferred to Chandigarh. Her husband is the only son of his parents. His parents are staying in the Village. After marriage Ms. V got settled in Chandigarh. Within a year of her marriage, she had a daughter and after 2 years she was blessed with a son. At present, her daughter is studying in 8th standard and her son is in 6th standard.

After marriage, Ms. V joined her bank in Chandigarh, where her immediate boss who was married man with children, tried to pass sexual remarks at her. She never faced such a problem in her previous workplace. Passing sexual remarks became daily affair for her boss. He was 50 years old. He also demanded sexual favours from her side. But Ms. V refused his proposal bluntly. Her refusal made boss furious and he made up his mind to teach her a lesson. She did not talk to anyone at her workplace about her harassment. However, her boss made false allegations against her character. He portrayed her as a woman of loose character who can go any extent to serve her interests. There was lot of false propaganda against her at her workplace and all the male colleagues and subordinates supported the boss. No body in her workplace supported her. She felt miserable and could not concentrate on her work. She decided to report the matter to the higher authorities. The superordinate, however, manipulated the matter. He did not allow her to lodge the complaint. He misplaced her complaint and filed a complained against her. She was blamed as sex starved female who blackmailed superordinates in order to get favours. She realized, she could never get justice, as her boss is very powerful. In order, to get rid of this problem, she requested the higher authorities for her transfer.

After working for two years in Chandigarh, she was transferred to Shimla. She shifted there along with her children, but her husband continued to stay at Chandigarh as his job was not transferable. After one month of her joining, she came to know that her previous boss had spread rumours of her past at the new branch, which led to nuisance and disrespect for her. She was not given respect by the male supervisors, colleagues as well as subordinates in the bank at Shimla. She felt very upset. Her physical as well as mental health started deteriorating. She continued to tolerate disrespectful behaviour and later after one year, got herself transferred to Rajpura in Punjab.

Being Rajpura, near to Chandigarh, she got settled with her husband in Chandigarh. Her children had also started going to school at Chandigarh. In Rajpura, she worked for two years. These two years were also very miserable for her. Male colleagues did not show any respect to her and all sorts of rumours about her character and unsuccessful marriage was spread. She felt miserable with the behaviour of male staff members. They were torturing her mentally. She could not cope up with the stress in the job. She got so much disturbed that she had to consult a Psychiatrist. She continued to work with depressed state of mind, later got transferred to Chandigarh. She remained with one branch at Chandigarh for two years. She got transferred to another branch. She got promoted after six years. Her subordinates were promoted earlier than her.

Ms. V shared all the problems with her husband. She continued to get his support all the time. According to her, it was one single episode of sexual harassment, which made her suffer throughout her working career. She realizes that she did not succumb to the pressures of the male officer and it was all retaliation against her. He succeeded in spreading all sort of rumours about her and disturbed her mentally. She feels that she is a weak person and did not take any action against her perpetrator. It is for this reason she had to suffer so long.

ANALYSIS OF THE CASE STUDIES

For the purpose of having an in-depth understanding of the problem, it was decided to take up case analysis. These case histories may not be representative of the cases discussed in earlier chapters. On the other hand, they may be unique or even unusual in a number of ways. Each woman may perceive her situation as unique because women, who make formal complaints, face different circumstances as compared to women who don't complain. However, these cases share certain common experiences like fear of stigma, fear of retaliation, fear of loss of job, psychological as well as health-related problems. The subsequent analysis highlights their background, workplace environment, their relations with male colleagues, superordinates and subordinates, causes of harassment, steps taken to end harassment, psychological trauma faced by the victims and coping mechanisms adopted by the victims to face the harassment.

Background of the Cases

In order to know the background of the cases, different variables like age, marital status, caste, religion, education, occupation, income, etc. have been discussed.

Age

In the present study, there were six cases (Case B, K, T, S, P, V), who were above the age of 40 years and four cases, i.e. case J, E, M and C were in the age group of 20-35 years. Out of these cases, there were five cases (J, E, M, C, P) who faced sexual harassment at an early age at their workplace. Five cases (Case B, K, T, S, V) faced sexual harassment at later age, i.e. after the age of 30 years. Such findings indicated that sexual harassment could occur at any age. The age of women respondent varied from 21 to 49 years. As reported in majority of studies most of the victims of sexual harassment were young, in the case analysis majority of victims were middle aged women.

Marital Status

The analysis of case studies revealed that out of ten cases, only one case, i.e. Case J was unmarried. There were three cases, i.e. Case B, C and P who were widows. Remaining six cases (Case K, E, T, S, M, V) were married. All the married cases started working before marriage except one case, i.e. Case M. Out of three widows, two cases started working before marriage, i.e. Case B and P while Case C started working after the death of her husband.

All the married women had the support of their spouses. Case J who was unmarried got the support of her parents. Case C and P were widows belonged to poor segment of the society. Hence the question of social support from Kinsmen did not arise in their cases. These females were socially isolated as they did not have consistent contact with members of their family of orientation. Lack of support made them vulnerable to harassment.

Out of six married cases, one case, i.e. Case E faced sexual harassment before marriage and all the widow cases faced sexual harassment after the death of their husbands. Irrespective of marital status, women were sexually harassed at workplace. The quantitative data of the study presented that married women faced more sexual harassment at workplace. However, majority of the researches, Chappell and Maritino, (2000); Fuentes *et. al.*, (1988); Merit Systems Study (1981); U. S. Merit Systems Protection Board (1988) reported that single women are more prone to sexual harassment at workplace.

Caste

Out of ten cases, two cases, i.e. case C and P belonged to lower caste background. Seven cases (Case J, E, T, K, V, M and B) belonged to intermediate caste. Case B belonged to Upper caste. Such a distribution indicates that the problem of sexual harassment at workplace was prevalent in all the caste groups.

Religion

Religion is that force which influences our ideology, value system and behaviour pattern. Qualitative data indicates that there were seven cases (Case B, K, S, M, C, P and V) who were Hindus and three cases, i.e. Case J, E and T belonged to Sikh religion. Thus, it can be stated that qualitative as well as quantitative data of the study presented that Hindu women were more prone to the problem of sexual harassment at workplace in the present study since there was over representation of Hindu religion. It can be stated that there was no segregation among inmates on the basis of religion.

Education

Analysis of case studies showed that majority of cases were educated. Case B was Matriculate. Case K was a Post-graduate and a diploma holder in Library Science and Office Management. Case J was a Graduate and diploma holder from Airhostess Academy. Case E did Professional course in Nursing and Ph.D. Case T and Case V were Graduates. Case S was M.Ed. Case M was BCA. There were only two cases, i.e.

Case C and P, who were illiterate. Both educated as well as illiterate women were sexually harassed. Majority of women were highly educated. Women who possess more work experience and higher education qualification are at the greater risk of sexual harassment and victimization (Decoster *et. al.*, 1999). Findings of Fain and Anderton, (1987); Merit Systems Study, (1981) have shown that educated women are more prone to harassment. The quantitative data of the study also came out with the same findings.

Occupation

The qualitative data shows that there were five cases (Case E, B, K, T and V) that were working in the Government sector. On the other hand, there were five cases (Case J, S, M, C and P) that were working in private sector. There were two cases, i.e. (Case T and V) who were engaged in occupations of higher prestige. Case T was working in Police force and Case V was working in a public sector Bank. There were six cases, i.e. (Case E, B, K, J, S, M) who were engaged in occupations of medium prestige. Case E was working as a Deputy Director in a Government Office on contract basis. Case B was working as a Peon in a Government Office. Case K was working on Administrative post in University. Case J was a freelancer and was writing for Human Rights Magazine. Case S was a Teacher and Case M was working as a Call Support Associate in a Call Center. Two Cases, i.e. (Case C and P) were involved in menial and occupations of low prestige. Case C was working in an NGO as a peer educator and also as a sex worker and Case P was working as a maid servant. Such analysis indicated that, sexual harassment exists in all occupational groups in the society. However, it is more among the medium occupational groups.

The case analysis also depicted that there was only one case, i.e. Case S who was working in a workplace where number of females was more than males. Remaining nine cases, i.e. (Case B, K, E, T, J, M, V, C and P) were working where male-female ratio was equal or where male ratio was more. Majority of researchers, i.e. Gruber, (1998); Gutek *et. al.*, (1990); Loe (1996); Moss (1997) also assumed that women who work in highly sexualized environments are likely to experience more harassment.

Income

Income determines the social status of individuals. The results of qualitative data depicted that there were three cases, i.e. Case B, C and P, who were earning less than Rs. 5,000 per month. These women were widows. Case C and P were illiterate. Case C was earning Rs. 1500 per month as peer educator and earning remaining amount as sex worker. There were five cases who were earning between Rs. 10,000 to Rs. 15,000 per month, i.e. Case K, J, E, S and M. There were only two cases, i.e. Case T and V who were earning above Rs. 15,000 per month. Economic necessity emerged as one of the main reason for working by women in the lower social class. Women who depend solely on their wages to support themselves and their families are unlikely to take risk at work. Their reluctance to either confront or complain makes them easy prey for sexual harassment (Stambaugh, 1997). These findings are applicable to two cases, i.e. (Case C and P).

Family Composition

Out of 10 cases, eight cases (Case B, K, J, E, T, S, C and V) were brought up in nuclear families and it was only after marriage that Case E and S joined the joint families. Case E and P were brought up in joint families and they set-up nuclear families after marriage. Women of both nuclear and joint families fought against the problem of sexual harassment at workplace.

Education of Family Members

Education in its wider sense includes everything that exerts a formative influence upon an individual. In the present analysis, it is expected that education of family members can provide women with better suggestions and solutions regarding their problems. Out of six married cases (K, E, T, S, M and V), spouses of all cases were educated. One unmarried case, i.e. Case J also belonged to well educated family. All the widow cases (Case B, C and P) were living alone with their small children. They were not treated well by their kinsmen after the death of their husbands. Two widow cases, i.e. Case C and P could not take any action against the harasser. They were illiterate and were in lowly paid occupations. Even when they tried to fight against sexual harassment, they did not get justice. Further, absence of educated family members was a disadvantage in their case.

Working Environment

In the present study, an attempt has been made to know the work place environment.

Age at the Time of Starting Work

The qualitative data shows that there were two cases i.e. Case B and E who started working at the age of 18 years, Case B and E started working due to economic necessity. There were six cases who started working between the age of 20-25 years, i.e. Case K, J, T, S, M and V. Out of these, there was only one case, i.e. Case M who started working at the age of 21 years because of economic necessity. There were two cases, i.e. Case P and C who started working at the age of 14 years because of economic need and there was one case, i.e. Case C who started working at the age of 14 years because of economic need. They started working at tender age and continue to work after the death of her husband due to economic compulsions. So, it can be said that out of ten cases, five cases, i.e. (Case B, E, M, C and P) started working due to sheer survival.

Work Hours

In Government sector, women work for 8 hours, whereas in private sector, sometimes they have to work more than 8 hours, they have to work late as well as in shift duties. There were five cases, i.e. (Case J, S, M, C, P) who were working in private sector. Out of five cases, three cases, i.e. Case M, C and P were working at odd hours. Case C and P were uneducated and were engaged in lowly paid occupations. In Government sector, there was only one case, i.e. Case T who was working in the Police had to perform duties at odd hours. Such findings negate the results of those research studies that state women who work late or in shift duties are harassed more as compared to those who work at normal working hours

(Hemlatha and Suryanarayana, 1983). Qualitative analysis indicates that sexual harassment was prevalent even in those occupational groups where women were not staying late or working at odd hours.

Sexual Harassment

In the present study, an attempt was made to know the age of the cases at which they faced sexual harassment, characteristics of the perpetrator, type of sexual harassment, period of sexual harassment, action taken by the victims, support at workplace, consequences and physical and psychological effects.

Age at which Faced Sexual Harassment

For the present study, it is very important to know the age at which these cases faced sexual harassment at workplace. The qualitative data shows that there were four cases (Case J, E, M and P) that faced sexual harassment between the ages of 20-25 years. There were three cases, i.e. Case B, K and T who faced sexual harassment at the age of 40 and above. There was one case, i.e. Case C who faced sexual harassment at the age of 28 years, one case, i.e. Case V faced sexual harassment at the age of 31 years, one case, i.e. Case S faced sexual harassment at the age of 37 years. Results indicate that women of all age groups faced sexual harassment at workplace. But majority of victims were middle aged women. However the quantitative data of the study indicated that young women, i.e. between the ages of 25-35 years faced sexual harassment at workplace. Other researches, i.e. Fuentes *et. al.*, (1988); Merit Systems Study (1981); U.S. Merit Systems Protection Board, (1988) also mentioned that young women are more prone to sexual harassment

By Whom Cases Faced Sexual Harassment

The qualitative data of the present study presented that maximum cases faced sexual harassment at the hands of their Superiors. There was only one case, i.e. Case E who faced sexual harassment from her colleague. Remaining nine cases, i.e. (Case B, K, J, T, S, M, C, P and V) faced sexual harassment from their superordinates. Findings of the qualitative data, indicate that maximum harassment of women at work place was done by superordinates which coincides with the findings of Brackenridge and Fasting (2005); Coleus (1986); Fitzerald *et. al.*, (1988); Lindsey (1977); Varro (1980); Worsfold and McCann (2000); Zaitun (2001). Results of Qualitative analysis coincides with the findings of quantitative data in the present study.

Most of the harassment was done by the superordinates thus, making more difficult for the victims to take action against their superiors because of fear of retaliation.

The Harasser/Perpetrator

An attempt was made to find out about the harasser. There were three cases, i.e. (Case E, C and P) where the harassers were between the ages of 30-40 years. There was one case, i.e. Case M, whose harasser was 45 years old. There were three cases, i.e. Case K, J and V whose harassers were of 50 years. There was one case, i.e. Case T, whose harasser was 52 years old and one case, i.e. Case S, whose harasser was 55 years old. There was one case, i.e. Case B, whose harasser was 64 years old. Results indicated that harassers of the victims ranged from 30 to 64 years age group. All of them were married and had children. Such findings indicated more elderly men were engaged in sexual harassment. The findings of qualitative analysis coincide with the findings of Merit Systems Study, (1981); Pryor *et. al.*, (1995).

The harassers of Case E, J and V did not misbehave with other female workers whereas, harassers of Case B, K, T, M, S, C and P were misbehaving with other female workers also. However, other females did not react to their waywardness and continued to face harassment at hands of their perpetrators.

Type of Sexual Harassment

The qualitative data shows that there were four cases i.e. Case (K, J, E and T) who faced sexual explicit remarks from the harassers. There was one case, i.e. Case B who faced non-verbal conduct of sexual nature. There were two cases, i.e. Case M and V who were asked for sexual favours, Case M was asked for sexual favours in return of wages. There were two cases, i.e. Case C and P who were physically molested. These cases were illiterate and were engaged in lowly paid occupations. The results indicated that harassers started with the mild form of harassment, i.e. staring, winking or making lewd gestures. When the victim did not take any action, she was asked for physical favour and in the extreme cases the harassers even tried to molest the victim. Perpetrator of the harassment tried to judge the victim whether she resisted sexual advances and accordingly continued with their behaviour.

Period of Sexual Harassment

In the present study, there were three cases, i.e. Case B, K and S who faced sexual harassment for approximately 1 year and Case K and S were sharing their problem with their husbands' right from the beginning and Case B was sharing with her friend from the first day. There were four cases, i.e. Case J, E, T and M who faced sexual harassment approximately upto six months. Case J, being unmarried, shared her problem with her parents and Case E shared her problem with her colleagues. Remaining two cases, i.e. Case T and M shared with their husbands. There were three cases, i.e. Case C, P and V who faced sexual harassment for many years. Cases C and P did not share their problem with anybody and Case V shared her problem with her husband. In total, three cases, i.e. Case J, T, M were fighting their battle to get justice at the time of recording of these case histories. In the beginning, cases tried to solve the problem on their own because they were afraid of stigma and reprisals. Victims were ashamed or embarrassed about what happened to them and preferred to keep quite about it, often also because they were afraid of being labeled as either "Loose" women or "Frigid" women who could not take a joke. Results thus coincides with findings of Wijayatilake & Zackariya (2000).

The victims who complained against the perpetrators tried to solve the matter of their own. They either tried to avoid the situation like demanded for her own transfer or ignored the offensive behaviours. Victims complained against the perpetrators only when the situation was not in their hands. The findings coincide with the results of Grubber &

Smith (1995); Keashly *et. al.*, (1994) who report that victims most often manage their experiences by trying to avoid and ignore the offensive behaviours

Action

Out of ten cases, there were two cases, i.e. Case B and K who complained to higher authorities at the workplace and got the justice. There were two cases, i.e. Case T and M who lodged a formal complaint against the perpetrator were fighting case at the time of recording of case histories. There was only one case, i.e. Case S who first complained to higher authorities, when did not get justice, went to legal way and won the case. One of the colleagues of Case E complained to higher authorities and Case E got justice. There were three cases, i.e. case C, P and V who could not take any action against the perpetrator. Cases C and P were illiterate and were not aware of their rights. Case P approached a women's organization but without any results. Case V first complained to higher authorities but the matter was manipulated by the superordinates. After this she did not try to fight, as she was sure, she would not get justice because of her superordinate's manipulations.

Results indicated that women who had support of their family members and were aware of their rights were able to seek justice for them in spite of initial hesitation. It was also found that authorities in the Government organization were serious with regard to providing justice to the victims. As soon as the victims lodged formal complaint enquiry was held. Whereas, in the Private sector, authorities lacked political will to check the problem of sexual harassment. Victims also rely on different forms of social support from friends, family and co-workers (Richman, *et. al.* 2001), including support from more formal associations (e.g. community or religious organizations). There were three cases, i.e. (Case B, K and V) in the Government sector who had sexual harassment cell at their workplace. In spite of the sexual harassment cell in the workplace Case V did not get justice. Women engaged in private sector reported that there was no sexual harassment cell present at their workplace. Case C and P worked in unorganized informal sector and these women had no redress to their grievances.

Support at Work Place

The case analysis showed that there were only two cases, i.e. Case B and E who got help from their colleagues and subordinates. Remaining eight cases (T, S, V, J, M, K, C, P) did not get help from other colleagues and subordinates to handle the situation. On the other hand perpetrators could gather lot of support for themselves. Women workers were too scared to support the victims openly. They feared negative repercussions had they sided with the victim. Men sided with male perpetrator as they were under the impression that if they supported the female victim, it would encourage other females to raise their voice, which they would not want. Most of the cases, it was the victim who was blamed for the whole situation. Results coincides with the findings of Wijaytilake and Zackariya (2000); Zaituns (2001). Such findings clearly highlighted the prevalence of patriarchal ideology in the society where women are not treated at par with men. At workplace, they are treated as women first, then as a worker.

Consequences

All the cases admitted that they were afraid of stigma and retaliation. The period of trauma was very painful for all the victims. Facing the same person daily at workplace added to more disturbances for the victims. They could not concentrate on their work. Further, none of the culprit felt even sorry or guilty about his behaviour. They rather left an impression of vindictiveness. A large number of studies have found that women who report sexual harassment are doubly victimized: first when they are harassed and subsequently through the protracted and traumatic process of redress, the victim is blamed and stigmatized and her prospects of continuing work is affected (Devika & Kodoth, 2001). Women remain silent from fear of having the event trivialized (Srivastava, 1999, Tejani, 2004) or loosing employment (Srivastava, 2004, Chaudhury, 2007). Cases B, K, J, E, T, S, M, V fall in this category.

Many do not report sexual harassment simply because they do not know how to and whom to seek assistance from. Illiteracy and lack of understanding of information pose difficulties for women working in unorganized sector (ILO, 1997). Qualitative analysis indicates that Case C and P fall in this category.

Physical and Psychological Effects

In the present study, all the ten cases faced both physical and psychological effects due to sexual harassment at work place. Their physical symptoms included headaches, inability to sleep, tiredness, etc. and psychological symptoms included anger, fear, depression, anxiety, helplessness, etc. There was one case, i.e. Case V who had to consult a psychiatrist to live upto the working environment. Dansky and Kilpatrick (1997), argued that women who have experienced unwanted sexual attention or sexual coercion at some point during their careers are likely to experience depression and symptoms of post traumatic stress disorder. Findings endorse the results of other studies that reported various physical and psychological problems faced by the victims of sexual harassment, Crull (1982); United States Merit Systems Protection Board (1981), (1987).

CONCLUSION

Sexual harassment is all about expression of male power over women that sustain patriarchal relations. It is used to remind women of their vulnerability and subjugated status. In a society where violence against women, both subtle and direct, is borne out of the patriarchal values operating in society, force women's conformity to gendered roles. These patriarchal values and attitudes of both men and women pose the greatest challenge in resolution and prevention of sexual harassment. Results indicated that sexual harassment is still endemic, often hidden, and present in all kinds of organizations. Yet it is still not always viewed as a problem, which has to be systematically tackled. The issue is of concern for both women and the employers.

Sexual harassment is an expression of male power over women. Although number of women have started working outside their homes, but they are not given respect by male superordinates, colleagues as well as subordinates at workplace. Women have been socially conditioned from an early age to be passive, meek and tolerant whereas men are socialized to be authoritative and aggressive towards women. These social/cultural constraints do not allow men to be subordinate to women and follow the orders of a female superordinate. There are men who still consider women's place is to be at home. Society and personal influences what we are taught as children in regards to roles of females and males overflow into the workplace. The managers of today grow up in families where their mother's stayed at home and took care of the children. They are also taught that men are stronger and should be the leaders. These behaviour flows into the work setting. Men have traditionally held organizational power and supervisory positions whereas women are not allowed to rise in their professional life. They are likely to be employed in subordinate positions. Women feel they are invisible, isolated and irrelevant within an organization while men see them as sex objects. Thus men with power positions at workplace feel that they have the authority to harass women. Women feel excluded from power and socially isolated at workplace. This imbalance of power leads to sexual harassment of women at workplace. Further, Patriarchy also plays an important role in the Indian society. Women are to obey the orders of men. They are perceived as an object of enjoyment by men. They are first treated as women at workplace then treated as a worker. Women working in highly sexualized fields face more problems at their workplace. In the male dominated workplace, a woman's gender is a salient feature because of her singularity and distinctiveness. The perpetrators with power positions are not at all guilty of their behaviour. Rather, they have an attitude of vindictiveness. Further sexual harassed women hesitate to complain against the perpetrators because of the fear of stigma to be attached to them and fear of retaliation. Only educated women are aware of their rights and are able to fight against the perpetrators. Whereas, illiterate women are unaware of their rights and also do not know where to lodge a complaint against the perpetrator. Women with economic compulsions do not complain against the perpetrators as they do not want to loose their job. In spite of the fact that Government has made the law to have sexual harassment cell in every organization where women work, in most of the private organizations, sexual harassment cell is not present. So, there is no redressal for their grievances which further leads to the perpetuation of the problem of sexual harassment. Men who are affluent and have power, authority and prestigious job are not afraid of law even. By using their power, they get the case dismissed. Rather it is the victim who is blamed.

Sexual harassment has been recognized as most intimidating, most violating form of violence since long in countries like UK, USA and many countries have not only taken note of how degrading experiences of sexual harassment can be for women as well as employers but have adapted legislative measures to combat sexual harassment.

In India, it has been eleven years since sexual harassment was for the first time recognized by the Supreme Court as human rights violation and gender-based systemic discrimination that affects women's Right to Life and Livelihood. The Court defined sexual harassment very clearly as well as provided guidelines for employers to redress and prevent sexual harassment at workplace. While the Supreme Court has given mandatory guidelines, known as Vishaka Guidelines, for resolution and prevention of sexual harassment enjoining employers by holding them responsible for providing safe work environment for women, the issue still remains under carpets for most women and employers. Vishaka guidelines apply to both organized and unorganized work sectors and to all women whether working part time, on contract or in voluntary/honorary capacity. The guidelines are a broad framework which put a lot of emphasis on prevention and within which all appropriate preventive measures can be adapted. One very important preventive measure is to adopt a sexual harassment policy, which expressly prohibits sexual harassment at work place and provides effective grievance procedure, which has provisions clearly laid down for prevention and for training the personnel at all levels of employment.

The Patriarchal attitudes and values are the biggest challenge in implementation of any law concerning women in our society. Combating these attitudes of men and women and the personnel involved/responsible for implementation of laws and systems is most crucial in prevention of unwanted sexual behaviour. Preventing and avoiding sexual harassment involves all levels of employees/persons in any organization—employees and colleagues, management and bodies like trade unions. Most importantly it requires for the employer to act before a problem occurs. Along with legislative measure, support of family members, education, job status, determination of women, etc. can help the women to cope up with the problem of sexual harassment. Being a male dominated society, presence of a male in a women's life can also make the other male feel afraid. Power theory, Social/Cultural theory and Sex-Role theory work in combination in the present study to explain the existence and perpetuation of sexual harassment at workplace.

6

Conclusion

Sexual harassment at workplace has become a reality in the lives of working women. It is an extension of violence in everyday life and is discriminatory, exploitative, thriving in atmosphere of threat, terror and reprisal. The reason for selecting sexual harassment of women at workplace as a topic of research was that very limited research has been done in this area in Indian context. Whatever research has been done is limited to few exploratory studies done by NGOs. Further, these studies have not used any theoretical framework to highlight the causes and precipitatory factors for the existence of this problem. The purpose of the present study was to know the extent of the problem of sexual harassment of women at workplace in the society.

The present study was done at Chandigarh and a purposive sample of 200 respondents was collected. For the purpose of quantitative data, the women working in the private sector were interviewed, as literature clearly points out that the chances of sexual harassment are likely to be more in the private sector because of less legislative enforcement. In the present study, women working in varied occupations, namely, Doctors, Nurses, Administrative Staff, Receptionists,

Actresses, Waitresses, Journalists, Sweepers and Construction Workers, etc. were focus of analysis. Additionally, qualitative data in the form of 10 case studies of women working in both Private and Government sector were undertaken. In order to understand the problem of sexual harassment of women at workplace in a broader perspective, ten case studies were undertaken. For purpose of collecting cases snow balling technique was used. Thus, in the present study both quantitative and qualitative data were studied.

The present study was undertaken with following objectives, namely,

- To find out the profile of the respondents, their work environment and their relationship with male colleagues, superordinates and subordinates.
- To find out the incidence of the problem, i.e. to what an extent sexual harassment is prevalent among women at work place.
- To explore working women's perception about sexual harassment, whether their understanding of sexual harassment coincides with Supreme Court's definition.
- To find out the main precipitating factors responsible for the problem of sexual harassment.
- To uncover and explore the main factors that would affect women's decisions for lodging a complaint in case of sexual harassment e.g. women who are needy or single would hesitate to lodge a complaint.
- To find out the coping mechanisms used by women at workplace to handle the problem of sexual harassment.

Results have been presented in six chapters. The *First Chapter* of the study highlighted the problem of sexual harassment of women at workplace in India and abroad through extensive review of literature. In the present study the Supreme Court's definition of sexual harassment at workplace has been used. Further, methodology adopted by the researcher for the purpose of data collection has been elaborated. The purposive sample of 200 respondents was drawn belonging to different age groups.

The *Second Chapter* dealt with the demographic, socio economic and family background of the respondents. Majority of the respondents, i.e. 58.5 percent were in the age of 25-35 years. 17.5 percent of the respondents belonged to less than 25 years, 22.5 percent of the respondents were in the age group of 35-45 years and 1.5 percent respondents were above 45 years. In the present study, majority of the respondents, i.e. 47.0 percent were married. 38.0 percent were unmarried and 15.0 percent respondents were once married but at the time of study were single that included widows, separated or divorced. Among the married respondents there were 64.5 percent of the respondents who had up to two children and 27.4 percent of the respondents had up to four children. 8.1 percent of the respondents were without children. Further, 18.4 percent of the respondents had only male children. 11.4 percent had female children only, whereas, 70.2 percent of the respondents were blessed with both male and female children.

Caste system is one of the basic pillars of Indian Social Structure. In the present study, majority of the respondents, i.e. 56.5 percent belonged to upper caste. 24.5 percent respondents belonged to middle caste and 19.0 percent respondents belonged to low caste. Religious background of the respondents indicated that majority of the respondents were Hindus, i.e. 75.0 percent, followed by Sikh, i.e. 22.5 percent, 1.5 percent respondents were Christian and only 1.0 percent were Muslim. Out of 200 respondents, 19.0 percent respondents were illiterate. 12.5 percent respondents studied upto high school, 33.5 percent respondents were graduate and 35.0 percent respondents were post-graduate and above. Thus, majority of the respondents in the present study were found to be educated. There were 46.5 percent of the respondents who were working in the middle level of occupations. 33.0 percent of the respondents were in the upper level of occupation. 20.5 percent of the respondents were engaged in occupations of lower type. In the present study, 60.0 percent of the respondents had permanent job and 40.0 percent were engaged in part time job. There were 20.5 percent respondents who were in low income group, i.e. below Rs. 5000. There were 34.0

percent respondents belonging to high income group, i.e. above Rs. 20,000. 45.5 percent respondents were in medium income group, i.e. between Rs. 5000-Rs. 20000.

The data indicated that out of 200 cases, 146 respondents were living in the joint family and 54 respondents belonged to the nuclear family. In the present study, majority of the respondents, i.e. 85.5 percent belonged to small family size, 12.0 percent had large family size and 5 respondents were staying alone. Majority of the respondents had educated head of the family, i.e. 64.6 percent were Graduate and above, 8.2 percent studied upto high school. 27.2 percent were illiterate. With regard to economic status of the family of the respondents it was found that 46.3 percent belonged to the upper income group, 18.9 percent of respondents' family belonged to the middle income group and 22.0 percent belonged to the low income group. There were however, 12.8 percent of respondents whose head of the family were not working, thus had no income.

The *Third chapter* dealt with the working environment of the respondents and their relationship with male colleagues, superordinates and subordinates at workplace. Data indicated that 51.5 percent of the respondents started working at the age of 20-25 years. 33.0 percent started working when they reached the age of 25-35 years and 15.5 percent started working very early, i.e. before they attained the age of 20 years. In order to get the job, 56.5 percent respondents adapted the formal channels, i.e. advertisement and 43.5 percent respondents used informal contacts, i.e. personal contacts. In the present study, 41.5 percent of the respondents admitted that they started working because of the economic necessity. 26.5 percent respondents mentioned that they started working for fun sake, time pass. 20.0 percent of the respondents reported economic independence as the main reason and 12.0 percent of the respondents reported that they started working for their personal growth.

Regarding attractive features of the job, there were 41.5 percent of the respondents who found their job good as it fulfilled their requirements. There were 30.5 percent of the respondents who reported good atmosphere at workplace. 16.5 percent of the respondents could not report any attractive features of the job, 7.0 percent gave importance to less working hours and only 4.5 percent of the respondents reported that their workplace was in close proximity to their residence.

In the present study, 22.0 percent of the respondents got formal training at workplace, out of which 15 respondents were trained by male instructor and 25 respondents were trained by both male and female instructors. Only 4 respondents were trained by female instructors. There were 6 respondents who faced sexual harassment by the male instructors.

Regarding work hours of the respondents there were 23.5 percent respondents who were working in the shift duties; out of which 35 respondents were working frequently in the shift duties and 12 respondents were working rarely in the shift duties. With regard to travelling, only 18.5 percent of the respondents admitted that they were travelling for their work assignments. Out of which 26 respondents travelled rarely, 6 respondents travelled sometimes and 5 respondents travelled frequently for their office work. Results indicated that women were working in shift duties as well as travelling for their job requirements even though their number was very small.

In this chapter the relationship of women with males at workplace was also assessed. Analysis of data revealed that all the respondents had male subordinates, colleagues and superordinates. However, there were 7 respondents who did not have their male subordinates. An attempt was made to evaluate the relationship of working women with their male superordinates, colleagues and subordinates. It was found the respondents who had more uncordial relations with their colleagues, superordinates and subordinates were married and young, i.e. 25-35 years age group. Further, it was found that the women belonging to upper castes, Hindu group had more uncordial relations with males at workplace as compared to other caste and religious groups.

Difference regarding relationships with males at workplace could be seen between illiterate and literate respondents also. The respondents who were highly qualified, i.e. Post-graduate and above faced more uncordial relations with males at workplace as compared to illiterate respondents. The respondents working in the middle occupational category like Clerical jobs, Actresses, Nurses, etc. faced more uncordial relations at workplace irrespective of their status, i.e. colleagues, subordinates or superordinates.

Additionally, an attempt was also made to discuss the kind of treatment women get at workplace by their male colleagues, superordinates and subordinates. 72.5 percent respondents felt, they were not treated as superordinates at workplace by male subordinates. Majority of women also opined that they were not treated as more intelligent to males at workplace, whether it is colleagues, superordinates or subordinates. Majority of the respondents felt that they were treated inferior to males at workplace. They were also considered to be poor performers by males at workplace. Half of the respondents advocated that their superordinates and colleagues doubted their capabilities to perform their duties of their own; 82.9 percent reported that their subordinates showed no respect to them and held the view that females could never perform their duties of their own. 62.0 percent women reported that they were treated as show piece and women of easy moral by their male subordinates. Further, 82.9 percent women reported that their subordinates made them feel that working women get promotion because of their fair sex status.

There were two main objectives of the present study, i.e. to find out the incidence of the problem of sexual harassment of women at workplace and to explore working women's perception about sexual harassment which had been discussed in the fourth chapter. Results indicated that 27.0 percent respondents were sexually harassed by male colleagues, 34.0 percent were sexually harassed by male superordinates and 10.0 percent were sexually harassed by their male subordinates. Out of these harassed respondents 4 respondents were sexually harassed by male colleagues, superordinates as well as by subordinates.

Out of 54 respondents, who faced sexual harassment by the male colleagues, majority of the respondents, i.e. 66.6 percent were of 25-35 years age group and were married, i.e. 57.4 percent. Majority of respondents who faced harassment at workplace were educated, i.e. 29.6 percent and 38.9 percent belonged to middle level occupations. Out of 68 respondents who faced sexual harassment by male superordinates, majority of the respondents, i.e. 52.9 percent were of 25-35 years age group and were married, i.e. 60.3 percent. Majority of the respondents were educated, i.e. 36.8 percent and 42.6 percent worked in occupations of upper level. Out of 20 respondents who faced sexual harassment by male subordinates, majority of the respondents, i.e. 75.0 percent were of 25-35 years age, were single, i.e. 60.0 percent, were educated, i.e. 50.0 percent and belonged to middle occupational category.

To explore working women's perception about definition of the Supreme Court on sexual harassment different components of the definition were spread in the form of 17 statements. There are five main components, i.e. unwelcome remarks, verbal and non-verbal conduct of sexual nature, sexually visual material, unwelcome demands and physical contacts in the definition of sexual harassment at workplace given by the Supreme Court of India.

First component, i.e. unwelcome remarks constituted three statements:

- When a man passes sexually explicit remarks or comment to a woman at workplace.
- When a man cracks jokes with sexual connotations to a woman at workplace.
- When a man passes sexiest remarks on a woman at workplace.

The respondents' perception was recorded by comprising all the three statements. Out of 200 respondents, 11 respondents strongly disagreed with unwelcome remarks at workplace. 39 respondents disagreed with the statement, 37 respondents were undecided about the statement, 76 respondents agreed with the statement and 37 respondents strongly agreed that unwelcome remarks at workplace constitute sexual harassment.

Second component, i.e. Verbal and non-verbal conduct of sexual nature constituted three statements:

- When a man at workplace stares at a woman to make her feel uncomfortable.

- When a man makes offensive gestures in front of a woman at workplace.
- When a man makes kissing sounds to a woman at workplace.

Respondents' views were recorded by comprising all the three statements. Out of 200 respondents, only 1 respondent strongly disagreed with the statement. Whereas 26 respondents disagreed, 27 respondents gave undecided response, 96 respondents agreed and 40 respondents strongly agreed that verbal and non-verbal conduct of sexual nature at workplace is sexual harassment.

Third component, i.e. sexually suggestive visual material constituted three statements:

- When a man shows sexually explicit books/ magazines/printed matter to a woman at workplace.
- When a man shows sexually explicit cartoons/ poster/calendars to a female worker at workplace.
- When a man shows pornographic e-mails/sms/ screen savers to a female worker at workplace.

Respondents' views were recorded by comprising all the three statements. Out of 200 respondents, only 1 respondent strongly disagreed with sexually visual material at workplace. 10 respondents disagreed, 39 respondents gave undecided response, 124 respondents agreed and 26 respondents strongly agreed with the statement.

Fourth component, i.e. unwelcome demands or requests constituted four statements:

- When a man demands or requests for sexual favours in return of payment of wages from a female employee at workplace.
- When a man demands for sexual favours from a female employee at workplace and makes it a condition for employment.
- When a man demands for sexual favours from a female employee at workplace and makes it a condition for increment.

- When a man demands for sexual favours from a female employee at workplace and makes it a condition for promotion.

Respondents' views were recorded by comprising all the four statements. Out of 200 respondents, there were no respondents who strongly disagreed and disagreed with the above statements. Only 2 respondents gave undecided response, 7 respondents agreed with the statement and 191 respondents strongly agreed with unwelcome demands at workplace as sexual harassment.

Fifth component, i.e. Physical contacts constituted four statements:

- When a man brushes against a female employee at workplace.
- When a man pinches a female employee at workplace.
- When a man touches a female employee at workplace.
- When a man grabs a female employee at workplace.

Respondents' views were recorded by comprising all the four statements. Out of 200 respondents, there were no respondents who strongly disagreed or disagreed with all the statements related to physical contacts. Only 2 respondents gave undecided response, 8 respondents agreed with the statement and 190 respondents strongly agreed with physical contacts as sexual harassment at workplace. Results show that respondents' perception about sexual harassment coincided with the Supreme Court's definition.

The *Fourth Chapter* also highlighted the problems, reasons, action, measures etc. for sexual harassment. The respondents were further asked to specify harassment of other female workers at workplace. 146 respondents reported that they were witness to harassment of other female workers at their workplace. Additionally, reactions of the respondents to sexual harassment of other females at workplace were assessed. Out of 146 respondents, 39.7 percent mentioned that they motivated the victim to take action against the perpetrator.

31.5 percent respondents remained mute spectators and 28.8 percent sympathized with the victim.

Majority of the respondents, i.e. 67.5 percent favoured active action like complaining to higher authorities, going to NGO's, filing police complaint, etc. by the victims and 32.5 percent favoured passive actions like ignoring the problem, leaving the job, etc. by the victims. Further, the respondents were asked about the type of punishment to be given to the perpetrator. Results showed that 34.5 percent respondents favoured police action against the perpetrator, 31.5 percent favoured public humiliation for the culprit; 23.5 percent favoured physical punishment; 10.5 percent mentioned suspension of the perpetrators from the workplace.

In the present study, an attempt was made to identify the characteristics of the victims. In this regard respondents were asked to specify the women who are more prone to sexual harassment at workplace. 25.5 percent blamed sexualized workplace environment as the main cause of sexual harassment of women. There were 23.0 percent respondents who mentioned economic vulnerability of the victim as the main cause of sexual harassment. There were 22.5 percent of the respondents who reported weak personality of the victims as a responsible factor for their sexual harassment, 11.5 percent blamed physical attributes of the victim, 9.0 percent blamed weak family background of the victim and 8.5 percent respondents referred high qualification of women as a main cause of harassment against her.

Respondents were also questioned regarding reasons for existence of sexual harassment in the society. Out of 200 respondents, 31.5 percent blamed underreporting of the cases as the main reason for perpetuation of sexual harassment. There were 26.0 percent respondents who mentioned social stigma against the victim in the society as the main reason for existence of the problem. There were 23.5 percent respondents who blamed weak legal system, 10.0 percent respondents blamed both social stigma and poor legislations as reasons for the existence of sexual harassment in the society. There were 9.0 percent respondents who highlighted the negative role of media in perpetuation of the problem of sexual harassment.

Results of the present study indicated that out of 200 respondents, majority of the respondents, i.e. 69.0 percent admitted that they faced sexual harassment at their workplace during their working tenure. There were 12.0 percent respondents who faced discrimination on gender basis, there were 9.0 percent respondents who faced problem of work environment, 5.0 percent respondents faced economic problem and other 5.0 percent faced problem of overtime at workplace.

The sexually harassed respondents, i.e. 138 were further questioned about how they solved their problem. 31.8 percent respondents shared their problem with friends and office staff, 27.7 percent complained to the higher authorities, 21.7 percent respondents shared their problem with family members and 18.8 percent ignored the problem. It is interesting to mention that when sexual harassment was done by a male colleague, majority, i.e. 55.0 percent respondents blamed both males and females. On the other hand, if sexual harassment occurred through a male superordinate, majority of the respondents i.e. 87.5 percent blamed males only. Similarly, if sexual harassment occurred through a male subordinate, majority, i.e. 84.0 percent respondents blamed males only.

To get rid of the problem of sexual harassment at workplace, majority of the respondents, i.e. 31.0 percent advocated stringent laws and resocialization of women into aggressive personalities to handle the situation. There were 23.0 percent respondents who favoured stringent law. 21.5 percent respondents wanted changed role for women and 19.0 percent favoured support of family and friends. There were, however, respondents who wanted for proper socialization of men in order to end the problem of sexual harassment.

In the present study in addition to taking quantitative data of 200 working women, qualitative data in the form of 10 case studies of women was also undertaken with an objective to highlight subtle form of violence women faced and to highlight their coping mechanism. The *Fifth Chapter* covered all the 10 case studies and the analysis of these case studies. Analysis of case studies showed that out of 10 cases there were six cases that were above 40 years of age and remaining four cases were in the age group of 20-35 years. Analysis of qualitative data indicated that only one case was unmarried.

Three cases were widow and remaining six cases were married. Three cases belonged to Jat caste, two cases were Khatri, one case belonged to Brahmin caste, one case belonged to Baniya caste, one case was a Rajput and two cases belonged to Scheduled caste. Seven cases were Hindus and there were three cases that belonged to Sikh religion.

Two cases had never been to school, one case was Matriculate, one case was a Post-graduate and had diploma in Library Science and Office Management. One case did diploma in Air Hostess Academy and was a Graduate. One case did course in Nursing and was a Ph.D. holder. One case did BCA and one case was a Graduate and cleared the Bank Clerical Entrance Test. Spouses of all married cases were educated, one unmarried case also had educated parents, three widow cases were living with their children and their children were still studying. Out of 10 cases, eight cases were brought up in nuclear families and out of eight cases; two cases joined the joint families after their marriage. Two cases were brought up in joint families and they set-up nuclear families after marriage. In the quantitative data also more respondents were living in the nuclear families. Five cases were working in the Government Sector and other five cases were working in the Private sector. Three cases were earning less than Rs. 5,000 per month, five cases were earning between Rs. 10,000 to Rs. 15,000 per month. Two cases were earning above Rs. 15,000 per month.

Analysis of qualitative data showed that two cases started working at the age of 18 years. Six cases started working between the age group of 20-25 years and two cases started working at the age of 14 years. Four cases were working at odd hours. Out of four cases three cases were working in Private sector and one case was working in Government sector. All the ten cases were also analyzed on the basis of their age at which they faced sexual harassment. Four cases faced sexual harassment at the age of 20-25 years. Three cases faced sexual harassment at the age of 40 years and above. One case faced sexual harassment at the age of 28 years, one case at the age of 31 years and one at the age of 37 years. It clearly presented that women of all ages faced sexual harassment but majority were middle aged women. Out of ten cases, only one case faced sexual harassment from her colleague, remaining nine cases faced sexual harassment from their superordinates.

In the present study, an attempt was also made to know the characteristics of the harasser through qualitative data. There were three cases whose harassers were between the age group of 30-40 years. One case's harasser was 45 years old. Three cases harassers were of 50 years age and there was one case whose harasser was 55 years old. One case's harasser was 64 years old. Results indicated that harassers of the victims ranged from 30 to 64 years age group. All of them were married and had children.

Out of 10 cases, four cases faced sexual explicit remarks from the harassers. One case faced non-verbal conduct of sexual nature. Two cases were demanded for sexual favours. One case was asked for sexual favours in return of wages. Two cases were physically molested. The women who were illiterate and were engaged in lowly paid occupations were physically molested. There were three cases who faced sexual harassment for approximately 1 year and four cases faced sexual harassment approximately upto six months. There were three cases who faced sexual harassment for many years.

Married respondents were sharing their problem with their husbands' right from the beginning. Only one married case shared her problem with her friend from the first day. One case being unmarried, shared her problem with her parents and one case shared her problem with her colleague. Two cases did not share their problem with anybody as they were illiterate, were engaged in lowly paid occupations and were widow. There were two cases who complained to higher authorities at the workplace and got the justice. There were two cases who lodged a formal complaint against the perpetrator and were fighting case at the time of recording of case histories. There was only one case who first complained to higher authorities, when did not get justice, went to legal way and won the case. One of the colleagues of a case complained to higher authorities and she got justice. There were three cases who could not take any action against the perpetrator. Among these three cases, two cases were illiterate and were not aware of their rights.

The qualitative analysis showed that there were only two cases who got help from their colleagues and subordinates. Remaining eight cases did not get help from other colleagues and subordinates to handle the situation. Women workers were too scared to support the victims openly. All the cases admitted that they were afraid of stigma and retaliation. The period of trauma was very painful for all the victims. Facing the same person daily at workplace added to more disturbances for the victims. They could not concentrate on their work. Further, none of the culprit felt even sorry or guilty about his behaviour. They rather left an impression of vindictiveness. All the ten cases faced both physical and psychological effects due to sexual harassment at work place.

MAIN FINDINGS

Incidence

Out of 200 respondents, there were 54 women who admitted that they witnessed sexual harassment of other female workers at their work place. There were 69.0 percent respondents in the present study who experienced sexual harassment themselves. Such findings help us to conclude that the problem of sexual harassment against women is quite prevalent in the private sector. Findings coincide with the results of ILO, (2001): Kumar (2007), who advocated that sexual harassment is widespread.

Work Relations

It was found that majority of the working women had uncordial relations with their male coworkers. Women were poorly treated mainly by their subordinates. Both educated and illiterate women had uncordial relations at workplace but illiterate women were hesitant to report uncordial relations because of lack of support and fear of the loosing job.

Age

In the present study, it was found that young women, i.e. between the age of 25-35 years faced more sexual harassment at workplace because younger women are new in profession, holds low occupational level, usually unmarried, thus constituting a less powerful group. The findings of the present study coincide with the findings of Fuentes *et. al.*, (1988); Merit Systems Study, (1981); U.S. Merit Systems Protection Board, (1988). However, the qualitative analysis show that even aged women faced sexual harassment at workplace.

Marital Status

It was found that married women faced more sexual harassment at workplace in comparison to unmarried, divorced, widow or separated women. It was because married women are more vocal about their problems at workplace as they have support of their families and were not sole earning members of their families. Such findings negate the findings of Chappell and Maritino (2000); Fuentes (1988); Merit Systems Study (1981); U.S. Merit Systems Protection Board (1988). Whereas, qualitative data of the study presented that women of all marital status were sexually harassed at workplace.

Education

Women with higher education were found to be more prone to sexual harassment at workplace in the present study. It is argued that the educated women have more awareness thus they are more sensitive to sexual harassment behaviours and protective of their rights. Results of qualitative analysis also presented the same picture. Such findings coincides with the findings of Decoster *et. al.*, (1999); Fain and Anderton (1987); Merit Systems Study (1981). Whereas qualitative data of the study presented that women of all marital status were sexually harassed at workplace.

Occupation

The present study depicted that women working in middle level occupations faced more sexual harassment at workplace by male colleagues and subordinates because they would hesitate to harass the women of upper occupational level. Whereas, women working in upper level occupations faced more sexual harassment by male superordinates because they hold the power at workplace. Other researches also mentioned that women of middle level occupations faced more sexual harassment at workplace. (Chappell and Maritino, 2000; Malla, 2000; Zaitun, 2001). However, qualitative analysis showed that women of all occupations faced sexual harassment but majority of them were of middle level occupations.

Harassment by whom

Majority of the respondents in the present study were sexually harassed by their superordinates as they were in powerful position at workplace. The qualitative analysis of the study also gave the same findings. Different researchers gave the similar results. Brackenridge and Fasting (2005); Coleus (1986); Fitzerald *et. al.*, (1988); Lindsey (1977); Varro (1980); Worsfold and McCann (2000); Zaitun (2001).

Harasser's Characteristics

Quantitative data of the study indicated that harassers were mainly married, older in age, working in high positions and were with misogynistic attitude. Such findings coincide with the findings of Merit Systems Study (1981); Pryor *et al.*, (1995). The qualitative analysis of the study also presented the same picture.

Perception of Sexual Harassment

The present study indicated that majority of the respondents did not consider unwelcome remarks, verbal and non-verbal conduct of sexual nature and sexually visual material as sexual harassment They considered it to be daily affair for them. Whereas, unwelcome demands and physical contacts were considered as sexual harassment by the respondents. They took it as the severe form of sexual harassment.

Coping Mechanism

Majority of the respondents either ignored the problem or shared with family members or colleagues. Very few respondents complained against the perpetrators. Case analysis presented that all the married cases had support of their family. Illiterate women lacked proper guidance, they preferred to ignore the problem. Further, the fear of retaliation made them to suffer. It has been found in the present study that majority of the respondents' perception of sexual harassment coincides with Supreme Court's definition, yet awareness with regard to legislation was minimal. In India, legislative process is slow and expensive, therefore very few women opt for legal battle against their perpetrators to end their victimization. Findings coincide with results of ILO, (1997); Wijayatilake & Zackariya (2000); Jayashree (1999); Chaudhury (2007).

Complain

Majority of the respondents advocated that active action must be taken against the perpetrators. However, among the sexually harassed respondents there were only 27.7 percent respondents who themselves complained to higher authorities. Such results show that women who are the victims of harassment want to take strong action against their perpetrators but due to societal pressures, meekly suffer from humiliation in isolation. Case analysis also presents that victims first tried to solve the problem on their own and took action when the situation became unbearable. The findings coincide with the results of Grubber & Smith (1995); Keashly *et. al.* (1994), who reported that victims most often managed their experiences by trying to avoid and ignore the offensive behaviours.

SUGGESTIONS

- Comparative and evaluative studies can be done in Government and Private sector.
- The research can be done in highly sexualized workplaces, i.e. where number of men is more like Armed Forces, Police, etc. In such workplaces sexual harassment is a frequently occurring phenomenon.
- To know the other side of the story the research can be done on the other forms of sexual harassment, i.e. same sex harassment as well as female to male harassment.

CONCLUSION

The phrase sexual harassment was first used in the decades of seventies. In India, it was the ruling of the Supreme Court (1997) in the famous Vishaka Case that brought the problem of sexual harassment at workplace to the public consciousness. The present study helps us to conclude that problem of sexual harassment at workplace is quite rampant in the Private sector. Women have awareness about sexual harassment, they are in agreement with definition of the Supreme Court. They perceive that they are being harassed. They advocate strict action against the perpetrators but themselves succumb to the pressures of the society and do not report their own harassment because they fear retaliation by the harasser, it can jeopardize her position and possibility for advancement. In the present study, it was observed that women were not treated at par with men at workplace. They were first treated as women, then as a worker. Men have traditionally held the organizational power inherent in management and supervisory positions, whereas women are likely to be employed in subordinate positions. Men are naturally reluctant to relinquish this superior position of privilege. Furthermore, men are socialized into roles of sexual assertion, leadership, persistence, whereas women are socialized to be passive, submissive and sexual gatekeepers. In our society men are often stereotyped as being receptive to and welcoming of the sexual advances of women. In contrast, women stereotypically are not as receptive to and welcoming of the sexual advances of men. The present study supports the influence of workplace power and gender relations for the existence and perpetuation of sexual harassment at workplace.

Need of the hour is strong implementation of the laws and women to become bold so, that this problem does not go unreported.

APPENDIX I

With regard to unwelcome remarks, three statements were constituted on five point scale. A score of five was assigned to a response indicating strongly agree and a score of four was assigned to a response indicating agree. Those who reacted with 'undecided' responses were given the score of three. On the other hand, those who did not agree to unwelcome remarks, that is, they disagreed with the statements, they were given a score of two and those who strongly disagreed with the statement, they were given a score of one. In this way, total score of a respondent could range from 3 to 15.

TABLE A.1
Distribution of Scores Regarding Unwelcome Remarks

Score	*Frequency*	*Perception*
3	11	Strongly disagree
4	5	Disagree
5	9	
6	25	
7	8	Undecided
8	17	
9	12	
10	10	Agree
11	8	
12	58	
13	22	Strongly agree
14	6	
15	9	

N = 200

The scores were arranged into ascending series and distribution was done into five parts. Respondents with a score of 3 were labeled as strongly disagree with unwelcome remarks; scores ranging from 4 to 6 were labeled as disagree with unwelcome remarks; scores ranging from 7 to 9 were labeled as undecided; 10 to 12 as agree and scores ranging from 13 to 15 were labeled as strongly agree with unwelcome remarks. In other words, there were total 50 respondents who disagreed with unwelcome remarks as sexual harassment at workplace. 37 respondents were such who could not decide about the statements. They themselves were not clear whether it is sexual harassment or not. There were 113 respondents who agreed with unwelcome remarks as sexual harassment at workplace.

APPENDIX II

With regard to verbal and non-verbal conduct of sexual nature, three statements were constituted on five point scale. According to the response given, each statement was coded, for every 'strongly agree' response, score '5' was given, score '4' for the response of 'Agree', score '3' for the response of 'undecided', score '2' for the response of 'disagree' and score '1' for the response of 'strongly disagree'. In this way, total score of a respondent could range from 3 to 15 for the total sample of 200 respondents. The distribution of scores was formed and arranged in ascending series.

TABLE A.2
Distribution of Scores on Verbal and Non-verbal Conduct of Sexual Nature

Score	*Frequency*	*Perception*
3	1	Strongly disagree
4	3	Disagree
5	9	
6	14	
9	37	Undecided
10	28	Agree
11	21	
12	47	
13	27	Strongly agree
14	10	
15	3	

N = 200

Although scores could range from 3 to 15, but there was no score of 7 and 8. On the basis of total sample, scores were arranged into ascending series and distribution was done into five parts. Respondents with a score of 3 were labeled as 'strongly disagree' which means respondents who had score of 3, did not agree that use of verbal and non-verbal conduct of sexual nature at workplace is sexual harassment. Respondents who had score from 4 to 6 were labeled as 'disagree' which means respondents who had score in this range did not consider verbal and non-verbal conduct of sexual nature at workplace as sexual harassment. Respondents with a score of 9 were labeled as 'undecided' which means neither they agreed with the statements nor they disagreed. Respondents who had score from 10 to 12 were labeled as 'agree' which means they consider verbal and non verbal conduct of sexual nature at workplace as sexual harassment and respondents who had score from 13 to 15 were labeled as strongly agree which means they consider verbal and non-verbal conduct of sexual nature at workplace as sexual harassment.

APPENDIX III

With regard to sexually suggestive material, three statements were constituted on five point scale. For every strongly agree response, score '5' was given, score '4' for the response of 'agree', score '3' for the response of 'undecided', score '2' for the response of 'disagree' and score '1' for the response of 'strongly disagree'. In this way, total score of a respondent could range from 3 to 15. The distribution of scores was formed and arranged in ascending series.

TABLE A.3
Distribution of Scores on Sexually Suggestive Visual Material

Score	*Frequency*	*Perception*
3	1	Strongly Disagree
4	1	Disagree
6	9	
7	1	Undecided
8	4	
9	34	
10	12	Agree
11	18	
12	94	
13	14	
14	5	Strongly Agree
15	7	

N = 200

Note : No respondents with a score of 5.

The scores were arranged in ascending series along with their frequencies. There were no respondents with a score of 5, thus this score was not taken. Distribution of score was done into five parts. Respondents with a score of 3 were labeled as 'Strongly disagree' which means respondents who had score of 3 did not agree that showing sexually visually material at workplace is sexual harassment. Respondents who had score of 4 and 6 were labelled as 'disagree' which means respondents who had score of 4 and 6 did not consider showing sexually visual material at workplace as sexual harassment. Respondents with a score from 7 to 9 were labeled as 'undecided', which means neither they agree with the statements nor they disagree. Respondents who had score from 10 to 12 were labeled as 'agree', which means they consider showing sexually visual material at workplace as sexual harassment and respondents who had score from 13 to 15 were labeled as 'strongly agree', which means they give very high weightage to showing sexually visual material at workplace as sexual harassment.

APPENDIX IV

With regard to unwelcome demands, four statements were constituted on five point scale. Score '5' was given to every 'strongly agree' response, score '4' was given to every 'agree response', score '3' was given to every response 'undecided', score '2' was given to the response 'disagree' and score '1' to response 'strongly disagree'. In this way, total score of a respondent could range from 4 to 20 for the total sample of 200 respondents. The distribution of scores was formed and arranged in ascending series.

TABLE A.4
Distribution of Scores on Unwelcome Demands or Requests

Score	*Frequency*	*Perception*
12	2	Undecided
13	1	Agree
14	1	
15	2	
16	3	
17	2	Strongly agree
18	4	
19	26	
20	159	

N = 200

Although scores could range from 4 to 20, but there were no scores from 4 to 11. On the basis of total sample, scores were arranged into ascending series and distribution was done into three parts rather than five parts, because there were no respondents who disagreed or strongly disagreed with these statements. Respondents with a score of 12 were labeled as 'undecided', which means they could not give any response or were neutral. Respondents who had score from 13 to 16 were labeled as 'agree' which means they consider unwelcome or requests at workplace as sexual harassment. Respondents who had score from 17 to 20 were labeled as 'strongly agree', which means they gave very high weightage to unwelcome demands as sexual harassment.

APPENDIX V

With regard to physical contacts, four statements were constituted on five point scale. For every response 'strongly agree' score '5' was given, for every response 'agree' score '4' was given, for response 'undecided' score '3' was given, for response 'disagree' score '2' was given and for response 'strongly disagree' score '1' was given. In this way, total score of a respondent could range from 4 to 20. The distribution of scores was formed and arranged in ascending series.

TABLE A.5
Distribution of Scores on Physical Contacts

Score	*Frequency*	*Perception*
12	2	Undecided
14	3	Agree
15	2	
16	3	
17	2	Strongly agree
18	3	
19	6	
20	179	

N = 200

Although scores could range from 4 to 20, but were no scores from 4 to 11 and of 13. On the basis of total sample, scores were arranged into ascending series and distribution was done into three parts rather than five parts, because there were no respondents who disagreed or strongly disagreed with these statements. Respondents with a score of 12 were labeled as 'undecided', which means they were neutral in their opinion. Respondents who had score from 14 to 16 were labeled as 'agree', which means they consider physical contacts at workplace as sexual harassment. Respondents who had score from 17 to 20 were labeled as 'strongly agree', which means they gave very high weightage to physical contacts as sexual harassment.

APPENDIX VI

For every response 'strongly agree' score '5' was given, for every response 'agree' score '4' was given. For response 'undecided' score '3' was given, for response 'disagree' score '2' was given and for response 'strongly disagree' score '1' was given. This procedure was followed for all the 17 statements. In this way total score of a respondent could range from 17-85.

Sexual Harassment

Score	*Frequency*	*Percent*	*Valid Percent*	*Cumulative Percent*
(1)	*(2)*	*(3)*	*(4)*	*(5)*
50.00	1	.5	.5	.5
54.00	1	.5	.5	1.0
55.00	3	1.5	1.5	2.5
56.00	2	1.0	1.0	3.5
57.00	1	.5	.5	4.0
58.00	3	1.5	1.5	5.5
59.00	5	2.5	2.5	8.0
60.00	1	.5	.5	8.5
61.00	1	.5	.5	9.0
62.00	2	1.0	1.0	10.0
63.00	6	3.0	3.0	13.0
64.00	6	3.0	3.0	16.0
65.00	7	3.5	3.5	19.5
66.00	6	3.0	3.0	22.5

(Contd.)

TABLE (Contd.)

(1)	*(2)*	*(3)*	*(4)*	*(5)*
67.00	11	5.5	5.5	28.0
68.00	8	4.0	4.0	32.0
69.00	12	6.0	6.0	38.0
70.00	14	7.0	7.0	45.0
71.00	14	7.0	7.0	52.0
72.00	7	3.5	3.5	55.5
73.00	8	4.0	4.0	59.5
74.00	11	5.5	5.5	65.0
75.00	16	8.0	8.0	73.0
76.00	27	13.5	13.5	86.5
77.00	12	6.0	6.0	92.5
78.00	6	3.0	3.0	95.5
79.00	2	1.0	1.0	96.5
80.00	4	2.0	2.0	98.5
81.00	2	1.0	1.0	99.5
85.00	1	.5	.5	100.0
Total	200	100.0	100.0	

Although scores could range from 17 to 85, but there were no scores from 17 to 49 and 51 to 53. Q1 emerged on the score of 67 thus respondents who had score below 67 considered sexual harassment as a low form of sexual harassment. Q3 emerged on the score of 71, thus respondents who had score from 68 to 71, agreed that it is medium form of sexual harassment and respondents who had score from 72 to 85, strongly agreed that it is the high form of sexual harassment.

APPENDIX VII

INTERVIEW SCHEDULE

1.0 Preliminary Identification

1.1 Address of the respondent

1.2 Age (in years)
- 1.2.1 Below 25
- 1.2.2 25-35
- 1.2.3 35-45
- 1.2.4 Above 45

1.3 Marital Status
- 1.3.1 Never Married
- 1.3.2 Married
- 1.3.3 Once Married

1.4 Caste

1.5 Religion
- 1.5.1 Hindu
- 1.5.2 Sikh
- 1.5.3 Muslim
- 1.5.4 Christian

1.6 Educational Qualification
- 1.6.1 Illiterate
- 1.6.2 High school
- 1.6.3 Graduate
- 1.6.4 Post-graduate and above

1.7 Present Family Composition
- 1.7.1 Nuclear
- 1.7.2 Joint/Extended

1.8 Household Composition:

Relation to Self	*No. of family members*	*Sex*	*Education*	*Occupation*	*Income*

2.0 Job History and Details

2.1 Occupation

2.2 Nature of Job

- 2.2.1 Part Time
- 2.2.2 Permanent

2.3 What is your approximate monthly income (in Rs.)?

- 2.3.1 Below 5000
- 2.3.2 5000-20,000
- 2.3.3 Above 20,000

2.4 At what age (in Yrs.) you started working?

- 2.4.1 Below 20
- 2.4.2 20-25
- 2.4.3 25-35

2.5 How did you get this job?

- 2.5.1 Formal
- 2.5.2 Informal

2.6 Why are you working?

- 2.6.1 Necessity
- 2.6.2 Economic Independence
- 2.6.3 Personal Development
- 2.6.4 Miscellaneous

2.7 Which of the attributes attracted you to opt for this job?

- 2.7.1 Money
- 2.7.2 Good Working Atmosphere
- 2.7.3 Less Working Hours

2.7.4 Workplace in Close Proximity
2.7.5 Miscellaneous

2.8 Did you receive any formal training after joining this job?

Yes/No

2.8.1 If yes, who trained you?
Male/Female/Both

2.8.1.1. If trained by male, did you experience any difficulty while being trained by male instructor?

Yes/No

2.9 What is your number of work hours?
2.9.1 Less than 8
2.9.2 8-12

2.10 Do you work in shift duties?

Yes/No

2.10.1 If yes, how often
2.10.1.1 Rarely
2.10.1.2 Frequently

2.11 Do you travel for your work assignments?

Yes/No

2.11.1 If yes, how often?
2.11.1.1 Rarely
2.11.1.2 Frequently
2.11.1.3 Sometimes

3.0 Relationship with males at workplace

3.1 How many male members are there at your work place?

	Superordinates	*Subordinates*	*Colleagues*
3.1.1	1-2	1-2	1-2
3.1.2	2-5	2-5	2-5
3.1.3	5+	5 +	5+

3.2 What type of relationship you have with your male colleagues at workplace?
3.2.1 Cordial
3.2.2 Normal
3.2.3 Uncordial

3.3 Treatment given by male colleagues at workplace?

3.3.1 They treat you as their equals.
Yes/No/Undecided

3.3.2 They treat you as more intelligent to male colleagues?
Yes/No/Undecided

3.3.3 They treat you inferior to male colleagues?
Yes/No/Undecided

3.3.4 They feel that you get the same salary but don't perform the same type of tasks as male colleagues?
Yes/No/Undecided

3.3.5 They feel that you can perform your different duties of your own?
Yes/No/Undecided

3.3.6 They are of the opinion that you are only show piece in the work place?
Yes/No/Undecided

3.3.7 They are of the opinion that you are of easy moral?
Yes/No/Undecided

3.3.8 They feel that you get promotions just because you are females?
Yes/No/Undecided

3.4 What type of relationship you have with your male superordinates at work place?

3.4.1 Cordial

3.4.2 Normal

3.4.3 Uncordial

3.5 Treatment given by male superordinates at workplace?

3.5.1 They treat males and females equal in the work place?
Yes/No/Undecided

3.5.2 They treat male colleagues more intelligent to female colleagues?
Yes/No/Undecided

3.5.3 They treat females inferior to male colleagues?
Yes/No/Undecided

3.5.4 They treat females inferior to male colleagues?
Yes/No/Undecided

3.5.5 They feel that females can perform their different duties of their own?

Yes/No/Undecided

3.5.6 They feel that not males but females are only showpiece in the workplace?

Yes/No/Undecided

3.5.7 They are of the opinion that female workers are of easy moral?

Yes/No/Undecided

3.5.8 They give promotions to females according to their capabilities?

Yes/No/Undecided

3.6 What type of relationship you have with your male subordinates at workplace?

3.6.1 Cordial

3.6.2 Normal

3.6.3 Uncordial

3.7 Treatment given by male subordinates at workplace?

3.7.1 They treat you as their superordinates?

Yes/No/Undecided

3.7.2 They treat themselves more intelligent to you?

Yes/No/Undecided

3.7.3 They treat you inferior to themselves?

Yes/No/Undecided

3.7.4 They feel that you get heavy salary but don't perform the tasks as required?

Yes/No/Undecided

3.7.5 They feel that you can perform your different duties of your own?

Yes/No/Undecided

3.7.6 They feel that you are only showpiece in the work place?

Yes/No/Undecided

3.7.7 They are of the opinion that you are of easy moral?

Yes/No/Undecided

3.7.8 They feel that you get promotions just because you are females?

Yes/No/Undecided

3.8 Have you ever been witness/heard about harassment of female workers at your workplace?

Yes/No

3.8.1 If yes, what did you do?

3.8.1.1 Mute spectator

3.8.1.2 Sympathize her

3.8.1.3 Motivated for action

3.9 What action, according to you should be taken by the victim?

3.9.1 Passive

3.9.2 Active

3.10 What punishment according to you, should be given to the culprit?

3.10.1 Public humiliation

3.10.2 Physical punishment

3.10.3 Police action

3.10.4 Suspension

3.11 In your opinion, which women are sexually harassed?

3.11.1 Physical attributes

3.11.1.1 Young

3.11.1.2 Beautiful

3.11.2 Personality traits of women

3.11.2.1 Having more education

3.11.2.2 Women themselves consider responsible

3.11.2.3 Afraid of reprisals

3.11.3 Poor legislations

3.11.4 Weak family background

3.11.4.1 No family support

3.11.4.2 Member of minority

3.11.5 Workplace environment

3.11.5.1 Women supervised by someone of opposite sex

3.11.5.2 Working in highly sexualized fields

3.11.5.3 Working at odd hours

3.12 Reasons for existence of sexual harassment in the society?

3.12.1 It goes unreported

3.12.2 Social stigma

3.12.3 Legal system is very weak

3.12.4 Role of media
3.12.5 Stigma and poor legislation

3.13 What type of problems do you face at work place?
3.13.1 Economic.
3.13.2 Over time
3.13.3 Discrimination
3.13.4 Sexual harassment
3.13.5 Any other

3.14 Have you ever faced sexual harassment by a male colleague at your workplace ?

Yes/No

3.15 Have you ever faced sexual harassment by a male superordinate at your work place?

Yes/No

3.16 Have you ever faced sexual harassment by a male subordinate at your work place?

Yes/No

3.17 How did you rectify your problem of sexual harassment?
3.17.1 Ignore the problem
3.17.2 Share with family members
3.17.3 Share with friends and office staff
3.17.4 Complain to higher official

3.18 If a woman is sexually harassed by a male colleague at workplace, whom you consider responsible?
3.18.1 Female
3.18.2 Male
3.18.3 Both

3.19 If a woman is sexually harassed by a male superordinate at workplace, whom you consider responsible?
3.19.1 Female
3.19.2 Male
3.19.3 Both

3.20 If a woman is sexually harassed by a male subordinate at workplace, whom you consider responsible?
3.20.1 Female
3.20.2 Male
3.20.3 Both

3.21 What measures you suggest to check this problem?
3.21.1 Law should be more stringent
3.21.2 Women to become more bold

3.21.3 Proper socialization of men
3.21.4 Support of family members and friends
3.21.5 Stringent law and bold role of women

4.0 Sexual harassment means

4.0.1 Unwelcome remarks

4.0.1.1 When a man passes sexually explicit remarks or comments to a woman at workplace.

Strongly agree/Agree/Undecided/Disagree/Strongly disagree

4.0.1.2 When a man cracks jokes with sexual connotations to a woman at workplace?

Strongly agree/Agree/Undecided/Disagree/Strongly disagree

4.0.1.3 When a man passes sexist remarks on a woman at workplace

Strongly agree/Agree/Undecided/Disagree/Strongly disagree

4.0.2 Verbal and non verbal conduct of sexual nature

4.0.2.1 When a man at workplace stares at a woman to make her uncomfortable

Strongly agree/Agree/Undecided/Disagree/Strongly disagree

4.0.2.2 When a man makes offensive gestures in front of a woman at workplace

Strongly agree/Agree/Undecided/Disagree/Strongly disagree

4.0.2.3 When a man makes kissing sounds to a woman at workplace

Strongly agree/Agree/Undecided/Disagree/Strongly disagree

4.0.3 Sexually suggestive visual material

4.0.3.1 When a man shows sexually explicit books/magazines/Printed matter to a woman at workplace

Strongly agree/Agree/Undecided/Disagree/Strongly disagree

4.0.3.2 When a man shows sexually explicit cartoons/Posters/Calenders to a female worker at workplace

Strongly agree/Agree/Undecided/ Disagree/Strongly disagree

4.0.3.3 When a man shows pornographic e-mails/sms/Screen savers to a female worker at workplace

Strongly agree/Agree/Undecided/ Disagree/Strongly disagree

4.0.4 Unwelcome demands or requests

4.0.4.1 When a man demands or requests for sexual favours in return of payment of wages from a female employee at workplace

Strongly agree/Agree/Undecided/ Disagree/Strongly disagree

4.0.4.2 When a man demands for sexual favours from a female employee at workplace and makes it a condition for employment

Strongly agree/Agree/Undecided/ Disagree/Strongly disagree

4.0.4.3 When a man demands for sexual favours from a female employee at workplace and makes it a condition for increment

Strongly agree/Agree/Undecided/ Disagree/Strongly disagree

4.0.4.4 When a man demands for sexual favours from a female employee at workplace and makes it a condition for promotion

Strongly agree/Agree/Undecided/ Disagree/Strongly disagree

4.0.5 Physical contacts

4.0.5.1 When a man brushes against a female employee at workplace

Strongly agree/Agree/Undecided/ Disagree/Strongly disagree

4.0.5.2 When a man pinches a female employee at workplace

Strongly agree/Agree/Undecided/Disagree/Strongly disagree

4.0.5.3 When a man touches a female employee at workplace

Strongly agree/Agree/Undecided/Disagree/Strongly disagree

4.0.5.4 When a man grabs a female employee at workplace

Strongly agree/Agree/Undecided/Disagree/Strongly disagree

Bibliography

Baird, C.L., Bensko, N.L., Bell, P.A., Viney, W. and Woody, W.D. (1995). "Gender Influence on Perceptions of Hostile Environment Sexual Harassment" cited by Julie Holiday Wayne, Christine M. Riordan, and Kecia M. Thomas (2001), "Is all Sexual Harassment Viewed the same? Mock Juror Decisions in same and cross gender cases". *Journal of Applied Psychology*, Vol. 86, No. 2.

Bardhan, K. (1985). "Women's Work Welfare and Status: Forces of Tradition and Change in India". *Economic and Political Weekly*, 20 (50).

Barr, P.A. (1993). "Perceptions of Sexual Harassment". *Sociological Inquiry*, 63, pp. 460-70.

Bennett Alexander, D. (1995). "Same Gender Sexual Harassment" cited by Julie Holiday Wayne, Christine M. Riordan, and Kecia M. Thomas (2001), "Is all Sexual Harassment Viewed the Same? Mock Juror decisions in same and cross gender cases". *Journal of Applied Psychology*, Vol. 86, No. 2.

Biaggio, M.K., Walls, D., Brownell, A. (1990). "Addressing sexual harassment: strategies for prevention and change". In Paludi, M.A. (Ed.) Ivory power: Sexual Harassment on Campus. Albany, NY: State University of New York Press.

Bjorkquist, K., Osterman, K., Hjelt Back, M. (1994). "Aggression among University Employees". *Aggressive Behaviour*, Vol. 20, No. 3, pp. 173-84.

Blakely, G.L., Blakely, E.H., Moorman, R.H. (1995). "The Relationship between Gender, Personal Experience, and Perceptions of Sexual Harassment in the Workplace". *Employee Responsibilities and Rights Journal*, Vol. 8, No. 4, pp. 263-74.

Boland, Mary L. (2002). Sexual Harassment: Your Guide to Legal Action. Naperville, Illinois: Sphinx Publishing.

Bowes-Sperry, L., Tata, J., Luthar, H.K. (2002). "Comparing Sexual Harassment to other forms of Workplace Aggression". In Sagie, A., Koslowsky, M., Stashevsky, S. (Eds.), Misbehaviour Disfunctional Attitudes in Organizations. New York: Palgrave/Macmillan.

Brasler, S.J. and Thacker, R. (1993). "Four Point Plan helps Solve Harassment Problem". *H.R. Magazine*, Vol. 38, No. 8, pp. 117-24.

Bularzik, Mary (1978). "Sexual Harassment at the Workplace: Historical notes", cited in Russell, Diana, E.H., Sexual Exploitation : Rape, Child Sexual abuse and Workplace Harassment (1984), Beverly Hills, Sage Publishers.

Caplow, Theodore (1973). Sociology of Work, Minneapolis, University of Minnesota Press.

Chappel, D. and Di Martino, V. (2000). Violence at Work, ILO, Geneva, IInd edition.

Chaudhuri, Paramita (2007). Experiences of Sexual Harassment of Women Health Workers in Four Hospitals in Kolkata, India, cited in www.rhm-elsevier.com.

Clarke, L.W. (1988). "Women Supervisors Experience Sexual Harassment, too". In Rose, S. and Larwood, L. (Eds.) Women's Careers: Pathways and Pitfalls. New York; Praeger.

Cleveland, J.N. and Kurst, M.E. (1993). "Sexual Harassment and Perceptions of Power: An under Articulated Relationship". *Journal of Vocational Behaviour*, Vol. 42, No. 1, pp. 49-67.

Coles, F.S. (1986). "Forced to Quit: Sexual Harassment Complaints and Agency Responses" cited by Kimberly T. Schneider, Suzanne Swan, and Louise F. Fitzgerald (1997), "Job-related Psychological Effects of Sexual Harassment in the Workplace: Empirical Evidence from two

Organizations". *Journal of Applied Psychology,* Vol. 82, No. 1.

Collier, B., and Williams, L. (1981). "Towards a Bilateral Model of Sexism" cited by Julie Holiday Wayne, Christine M. Riordan, and Kecia M. Thomas (2001), "Is all sexual harassment viewed the same? Mock Juror decisions in same and cross gender cases". *Journal of Applied Psychology,* Vol. 86, No. 2.

Combat Law (2003). "The Human Rights Magazine", Special issue on Violence against Women, September-October.

Crull, P. (1982). "Stress effects of sexual harassment on the job: Implications for counseling" cited by Kimberly T. Schneider, Suzanne Swan, and Louise F. Fitzgerald (1997), "Job-related Psychological Effects of Sexual Harassment in the Workplace: Empirical evidence from two Organizations". *Journal of Applied Psychology,* Vol. 82, No. 1.

Dalal, S. (2003). "Bias in the Boardroom". *The Sunday Express,* May 18.

Danish-Gallup Institute (1991). Survey of approximately 1,350 Women, Copenhagen by Date-Bah, Eugine (1997) in Promoting Gender Equality at Work: Turning Vision into Reality for the Twenty-first Century. London: Zed Bks.

Dansky, B.S., and Kilpatrick, D.G. (1997). "Effects of Sexual Harassment" cited by Kimberly T. Schneider, Suzanne Swan, and Louise F. Fitzgerald (1997), "Job-related Psychological Effects of Sexual Harassment in the Workplace: Empirical Evidence from two Organizations". *Journal of Applied Psychology,* Vol. 82, No. 1.

Decoster, S., Estes, S.B. and Mueller, C.W. (1999). "Routine Activities and Sexual Harassment in the Workplace". *Work and Occupations,* Vol. 26, No. 1, pp. 21-43.

Defour, D. (1990). "The Interface of Racism and Sexism on College Campuses". In M. Paludi (Ed.). The Ivory Tower: Sexual Harassment on Campus, Albany: University of New York Press.

Devi, Lalitha (1982). Status and Employment of Women in India. New Delhi, B.R. Publishing Corporation.

Devika, J. and Kodoth, P. (2001). "Sexual Violence and Predicament of Feminist Politics in Kerala", *Economic and Political Weekly*, August 18, No. 18.

Di Tomaso, N. (1991). "Sexuality in the Workplace: Discrimination and Harassment". In J. Hearn, D.L. Sheppard, P. Tancred-Sheriff, G. Burrell (Eds.), *The Sexuality of Organization*, Beverly Hills, CA: Sage.

Dzeich, B.W. and Weiner, L. (1990). The Lecherous Professor : Sexual Harassment on Campus. Chicago, Illinois : University of Illinois Press.

Equal Employment Opportunity Commission (1980). "Guidelines on Discrimination because of Sex". Federal Register, 65, 74.

Equal Employment Opportunity Commission (1998). "Sexual harassment charges" cited by Julie Holiday Wayne, Christine M. Riordan, and Kecia M. Thomas (2001), "Is all Sexual Harassment viewed the same? Mock Juror decisions in same and cross gender cases". *Journal of Applied Psychology*, Vol. 86, No. 2.

European Commission (1999). "Sexual Harassment in the Workplace in the European Union". Report published by European Commission, Director General for Employment, *Industrial Relations and Social Affairs*, Luxembourg.

Fain, T.C. and Anderton, D.L. (1987). "Sexual Harassment: Organizational Context and Diffuse Status". *Sex Roles*, Vol. 17, No. 5, pp. 291-311.

Farley, L. (1978). "Sexual Shakedown : The Sexual Harassment of Women on the Job", cited in Russell, Diana, E.H. (1984), Sexual Exploitation: Rape, Child Sexual Abuse and Workplace Harassment, Beverly Hills, Sage Publishers.

Firestone, J.M. and Harris, R.J. (1997). "Organizational Climate, Leadership and Individual Responses to Sexual Harassment in the Active Duty Military". *Free Inquiry in Creative Sociology*, Vol. 25, No. 2, pp. 211-18.

Fiske, S. and Neuberg, S.A. (1990). "The Ecology of Diversity in Organizational Meetings: Lessons from a Case Study" cited in *Human Relations*, Vol. 5, 1998, pp. 589-623, available on hum.sagepub.com/cgi/content/refs/51/5/589.

Fitgzerald, L.F., Gelfand, M.J., and Drasgow, F. (1995). "Measuring Sexual Harassment: Theoretical and Psychometric advances". *Basic and Applied Social Psychology*, Vol. 17, No. 4, pp. 425-45.

Fitgzerald, L.F., Shullman, S.L., Bailey, N., Richards, M., Swecker, J., Gold, Y., Ormerod, M. and Weitzman, L. (1988). "The Incidence and Dimensions of Sexual Harassment in Academia and the Workplace". *Journal of Vocational Behaviour*, Vol. 32, No. 2, pp. 152-75.

Fitzgerald, L.F., Drasgow, F., Hulin, C.L., Gelfand, M.J. and Magley, V. (1997). "Antecedents and Consequences of Sexual Harassment in Organizations: A Test of an Integrated Model". *Journal of Applied Psychology*, Vol. 82, No. 3, pp. 578-89.

Fitzgerald, L.F. and Shullman, S.L. (1993). "Sexual harassment: A research analysis and agenda for the 1990s". *Journal of Vocational Behaviour*, Vol. 42, No. 1, pp. 5-27.

Fitzgerald, L.F., Drasgow, F., Hulin, C.L., Gelfand, M.J., Magley, V.J. (1997). "Antecedents and Consequences of Sexual Harassment in Organizations, A test of an Integrated Models". *Journal of Applied Psychology*, Vol. 82, No. 4, pp. 578-89.

Fuentes, M.C. (1988). "Discriminacryn y acosa sexual a la mujer en el trabajo (Discrimination and Sexual Harassment of Women at Work)". Cited by Date-Bah Eugenia (1997) in Promoting Gender Equality at Work: Turning Vision into reality for the Twenty-first Century. London: Zed Bks.

Glomb, T.M., Munson, L.J., Hulin, C.L., Bergman, M.E., Drasgow, F. (1999). "Structural Equation Models of Sexual Harassment : Longitudinal Explorations and Cross-sectional Generalizations". *Journal of Applied Psychology*, Vol. 84, No. 3, pp. 390-402.

Grauerholz, L., Gottfried, H., Stohi, C., Gobin, N. (1999). "There is Safety in Numbers: Creating a Campus Advisers' Network to help Complainants of Sexual Harassment and Complaint Receivers". *Violence against Women*, Vol. 5, No. 8, pp. 950-77.

Gruber, J. (1998). "The Impact of Male Work Environment and Organizational Policies on Women's Experiences for

Sexual Harassment". *Gender and Society,* Vol. 12, No. 3, pp. 301-20.

Gruber, J.E. and Smith, M.D. (1995). "Women's Responses to Sexual Harassment : A Multivariate Analysis". *Basic and Applied Social Psychology,* Vol. 17, No. 4, pp. 543-62.

Gruber, J.E. and Bjorn, L. (1986). "Women's Responses to Sexual Harassment: Analysis of Socio-cultural, Organizational and Personal Resource Models". *Social Science Quarterly,* 67, pp. 814-26.

Gutek, B. (1995). "How Subjective is Sexual Harassment? An Examination of Rate Effects" cited by Julie Holiday Wayne, Christine M. Riordan, and Kecia M. Thomas (2001), "Is all Sexual Harassment Viewed the Same? Mock Juror decisions in same and cross gender cases". *Journal of Applied Psychology,* Vol. 86, No. 2.

Gutek, B. (1985). "Sex and the Workplace" cited by Liberty J., Munson, Andrew G.M., and Charles Hulin (2001), "Labeling Sexual Harassment in the Military: An Extension and Replication". *Journal of Applied Psychology,* Vol. 86, No. 2.

Gutek, B., and O' Connor, M. (1995). "The Empirical basis for the Reasonable Woman Standard" cited by Julie Holiday Wayne, Christine M. Riordan, and Kecia M. Thomas (2001), "Is all Sexual Harassment Viewed the same? Mock Juror decisions in same and cross gender cases". *Journal of Applied Psychology,* Vol. 86, No. 2.

Gutek, B., Morasch, B., and Cohen, A.G. (1983). "Interpreting Social-sexual Behaviour in a Work Setting" cited by Julie Holiday Wayne, Christine M. Riordan, and Kecia M. Thomas (2001), "Is all Sexual Harassment Viewed the same? Mock Juror decisions in same and cross gender cases". *Journal of Applied Psychology,* Vol. 86, No. 2.

Gutek, B.A. and Koss, M.P. (1993). "Changed Women and Changed Organizations: Consequences of and Coping with Sexual Harassment". *Journal of Vocational Behaviour,* Vol. 42, No. 1, pp. 28-48.

Gutek, B.A. and Morasch, B. (1982). "Sex-ratios, Sex-role Spillover, and Sexual Harassment of Women at Work". *Journal of Social Issues,* Vol. 38, No. 4, pp. 55-74.

Gutek, B.A., Cohen, A.G., Konard, A.M. (1990). "Predicting Social Sexual Behaviour at Work: A Contact Hypothesis". *The Academy of Management Journal*, Vol. 33, No. 3, pp. 560-77.

Harris, R.J. and Firestone, J.M. (1997). "Subtle Sexism in the U.S. Military: Individual Responses to Sexual Harassment". In N. Benokraitis (ed.), Subtle Sexism: Current Practices and Prospects for Change. Beverly Hills: Sage.

Hartnett, J.J., Robinson, D., Singh, B. (1989). "Perceptions of Males and Females Toward Sexual Harassment and Acquiescence". *Journal of Social Behaviour and Personality*, Vol. 4, No. 3, pp. 291-98.

Hemlatha P. and Suryanarayana M. (1983). "Married Working Women: A Study on their Role Interactions". *The Indian Journal of Social Work*, Vol. XLIV, No. 2.

Hinde, R.A. (1979). Towards Understanding Relationships. Academic Press, London.

'Hindustan Times', 14 Sept., 2004.

Huda, S. (2001). "Study on Sexual Harassment in Bangladesh". Working paper for the ILO, Dhaka.

Hulin, C.L., Fitzgerald, L.F., Drasgow, F.D. (1996). "Organizational Influences on Sexual Harassment". In Stockdale, M.S. (ed.), Sexual Harassment in the Workplace: Perspectives, Frontiers, and Response Strategies, Thousand Oaks, CA: Sage.

ILO (1993). "A Comprehensive Women's Employment Strategy for Indonesia", Final Report of an ILO/UNDP TSSI Mission, Bangkok cited by Date-Bah Eugenia (1997) in Promoting Gender Equality at work: Turning Vision into Reality for the Twenty-first Century. London: Zed Bks.

ILO (1997). "Combating Sexual Harassment at Work". Conditions of Work Digest, cited by Date-Bah Eugenia (1997) in Promoting Gender Equality at Work: Turning Vision into Reality for the Twenty-first Century. London: Zed Bks.

ILO (2001). "Action against Sexual Harassment at Work in Asia and Pacific". Technical Report for discussion at the ILO/ Japan Regional Tripartite Seminar on action against

Sexual Harassment at Work in Asia and the Pacific, Penang, Malaysia, 2-4 Oct., 2001.

Inmania, Mary (1965). "Married Working Women: A Study on their Role Interactions". *The Indian Journal of Social Work*, Vol. XLIV, No. 2, July, 1983.

Jayashree, S. (1999). "Sexual Harassment at Work: an HRM perspective". *Indian Journal of Industrial Relations*, No. 1, pp. 202-16.

Kapur, Promilla (1974). The Changing Status of the Working Women in India. Delhi: Vikas Publishing House.

Keashly, L., Trott, V., MacLean, L.M. (1994). "Abusive Behaviour in the Workplace: A Preliminary Investigation". *Violence and Victims*, Vol. 9 No. 4.

Knapp, D.E., Faley, R.H., Ekeberg, S.E., Du Bois, C.L.Z. (1997). "Determinants of Target Responses to Sexual Harassment: A Conceptual Framework". *Academy of Management Review*, Vol. 22, No. 3, available on www.accessmy library.com/coms 2/summary-0286-292371 ITM.

Konard, A.M. and Gutek, B.A. (1986). "Impact of Work Experiences on Attitudes Toward Sexual Harassment". *Journal of Employee Responsibilities and Rights*, Vol. 8, No. 4.

Koss, M.P. (1987). "Changed Lives: The Psychological Impact of Sexual Harassment". In Paludi, M.A. (ed.) Ivory Power: Sexual Harassment on Campus. Albany, NY, State University of New York Press.

Kronenberger, G.K. and Bourke, D.L. (1981). "Effective training and the elimination of sexual harassment", cited by Perry, E.L., Kulik, C.T., Schmidtke, J.M. (1998) in "Individual Differences in the Effectiveness of Sexual Harassment Awareness Training". *Journal of Applied Social Psychology*, Vol. 28, No. 8, pp. 698-723.

Kumar, M.P. (2007). End to Harassment. Women's Feature Service. Ref. IND C 505 available on www.wfsnews.org.

Lach, D.H. and Gwartney-Gibbs, P.A. (1993). "Sociological Perspectives on Sexual Harassment and Workplace Dispute Resolution". *Journal of Vocational Behaviour*, Vol. 42, No. 1, pp. 102-15.

Langelan, M. (1993). Back Off: How to Confront and Stop Sexual Harassment and Harassers, cited in www.simonsays.com/content/book.cfm? tab=1 and pid=591444-36k.

Lawyers' Collective (2001). "Sexual Harassment at the Workplace: India Study Report". Working paper for the ILO, New Delhi.

Lengnik-Hall, M. (1995). "Sexual Harassment Research : A Methodological Critique" cited by Julie Holiday Wayne, Christine M. Riordan, and Kecia M. Thomas (2001), "Is all Sexual Harassment viewed the same? Mock Juror decisions in same and cross gender cases". *Journal of Applied Psychology*, Vol. 86, No. 2.

Livingston, J.A. (1982). "Responses to sexual harassment on the job: Legal, Organizational and individual actions". *Journal of Social Issues*, Vol. 38, No. 4, pp. 5-22.

Loe, M. (1996) "Working for Men—at the Intersection of Power, Gender and Sexuality". *Sociological Inquiry*, Vol. 66, No. 4, pp. 399-421.

Mackinnon, C. (1979). Sexual Harassment of Working Women. New Haven, Yale University Press.

Magley, V.J., Fitzgerald, L.F., De Nardo, M. (1992). "Labeling Sexually Harassing Behaviours as Sexual Harassment" cited by Liberty J., Munson, Andrew G.M., and Charles Hulin (2001), "Labeling Sexual Harassment in the Military : An Extension and Replication". *Journal of Applied Psychology*, Vol. 86, No. 2.

Mahajan, A. (1982). Indian Police Women. Delhi, Deep and Deep Publications.

Manohar, A. (2006). "Violence against Women: A Perspective", *Yojana*, A Development Monthly Magazine, October.

Marks, M.A. and Nelson, E.S. (1993). "Sexual Harassment on Campus : Effects of Professor Gender on Perceptions of Sexually Harassing Behaviour", cited by Julie Holiday Wayne, Christine M. Riordan, and Kecia M. Thomas (2001), "Is all Sexual Harassment viewed the same? Mock Juror decisions in same and cross gender cases". *Journal of Applied Psychology*, Vol. 86, No. 2.

Mathew, Mini (2002). Sexual Harassment at Workplace. India Centre for Human Rights and Law, Mumbai.

Merit Systems Protection Board (1981). "Sexual Harassment in the Federal Work Place: Is it a Problem?", cited in Russell, Diana, E.H. (1984), Sexual Exploitation : Rape, Child Sexual Abuse and Workplace Harassment, Beverly Hills, Sage Publishers.

Miller, L.L. (1998). "Feminism and the exclusion of Army Women from Combat". *Gender Issues*, 16, pp. 33-64.

Moss, J. (1997). "Lesbian Baiting in the Barracks, the Advocate", cited by Renzetti, *et. al.* (eds.) (2002) in Source Book on Violence Against Women. New Delhi, Sage.

Moyanahan, B. (1993). "Creating Harassment-free Work Zones". *Training and Development*, Vol. 47, No. 5, pp. 69-70.

Nadel, S.F. (1956). The Theory of Social Structure, London, Cohen and West Ltd.

National Crime Records Bureau (2006), "Crime against Women", available on http://ncrb.nic.in/cii2006/ home.htm.

O'connell, C.E. and Korabik, K. (2000). "Sexual Harassment: The Relationship of Personal Vulnerability, Work Context, Perpetrator Status, and Type of Harassment Outcomes". *Journal of Vocational Behaviour*, Vol. 56, No. 3, pp. 299-329.

Parikh, J.I. and Garg, K.P. (1987). "Training for Trainers: A Programme for Women Managers", cited by Parikh, I.J. and Shah, N.A. (1994), "Women Managers in Transition: From Homes to Corporate Offices". *The Indian Journal of Social Work*, Vol. LV, No. 2.

Park, A. (2007). U.S. Hotel and Casino Caesars Palace settles Sexual Harassment Lawsuit, available on www. Personneltoday.com/articles/ 2007/08/23/42040/us-hotel-and-casino-caesars-palace-settles-sexual-harssment_ lawsuit-with-427000-payout.html.

Parthasarathy, K. (1990). "Readings in Leadership and Self-Development Programme for Women Executives", cited by Parikh, I.J., Shah, N.A. (1994), "Women Managers in Transition: From Homes to Corporate Offices". *The Indian Journal of Social Work*, Vol. LV, No. 2.

Patel, Vibhuti (2002). Women's Challenges of the New Millennium, Delhi, Gyan Publications.

Peterson, Tashia (2000). "Action against Sexual Harassment at Work—A Malaysian Report", Working Paper for ILO, Kuala Lumpur.

Pierce, C.A. and Aguinis, H. (2003). "Romantic Relationships in Organizations: A Test of a Model of Formation and Impact Factors". *Management Research*, 1, pp. 161-69.

Pierce, C.A. (1998). "Factors Associated with Participating in a Romantic Relationship in a Work Environment". *Journal of Applied Social Psychology,* 28, pp. 1712-30.

Pradhan Malla, S. (2001). "Sexual Harassment at the Workplace in Nepal". Working paper for the ILO, Kathmandu.

Prasad, S.S. (1988). "Tribal Women Labourers: Aspects of Economic and Physical Exploitation", cited by Date-Bah Eugenia (1997) in Promoting Gender Equality at Work: Turning Vision into Reality for the Twenty-first Century. London: Zed Bks.

Pryor, J. and Mc Kinney, K. (1995). "Research on Sexual Harassment: Lingering Issues and Future Directions", cited by Julie Holiday Wayne, Christine M. Riordan, and Kecia M. Thomas (2001), "Is all Sexual Harassment viewed the same? Mock Juror decisions in same and Cross Gender Cases". *Journal of Applied Psychology,* Vol. 86, No. 2.

Pryor, J.B. and Day, J.D. (1988). "Interpretations of Sexual Harassment: An Attributional Analysis". *Sex Roles,* Vol. 18, Nos. 7-8, pp. 405-17.

Pryor, J.B., Giedd, J.L., Williams, K.B. (1995). "A Social Psychological Model for Predicting Sexual Harassment". *Journal of Social Issues,* Vol. 51, No. 1, pp. 69-84.

Pryor, J.B., Lavite, C.M., Stoller, L.M. (1993). "A Social Psychological Analysis of Sexual Harassment: The Person/Situation Interaction". *Journal of Vocational Behaviour,* Vol. 42, No. 1, pp. 68-83.

Rani, Kala (1976). Role Conflict in Working Women. New Delhi: Chetana Publications.

Richman, J.A., Rospenda, K.M., Flaherty, J.A., Freels, S. (2001). "Workplace harassment, Active Coping and Alcohol Related Outcomes". *Journal of Substance Abuse,* Vol. 13, No. 3, pp. 347-66.

Riger, S. (1991). "Gender Dilemmas in Sexual Harassment Policies and Procedures". *American Psychologist,* 46, pp. 497-505.

Rospenda, K.M., Richman, J.A., Wislar, J.S., Flaherty, J.A. (2000). "Chronicity of Sexual Harassment and Generalized Workplace Abuse: Effects on Drinking Outcomes". *Addiction,* 95(12). available on www. elsevier.com/locate/

socscimed.

Rotundo, M., Nguyen, D.H., Sackett, P.R. (2001). "A Metaanalytic Review of Gender Differences in Perceptions of Sexual Harassment". *Journal of Applied Psychology,* Vol. 86, No. 5, pp. 914-22.

Rubenstein, M. (1992). Preventing and Remedying Sexual Harassment at Work: A Resource Manual. London: Eclipse.

Samhita (2001). The Politics of Science. Kolkata, available on www.rhmjournal.org.uk.

Sandroff, R. (1992). "Sexual Harassment: The Inside Story". *Working Woman Magazine,* June, 78, pp. 47-51.

Sbraga, T.P. and O' Donohue, W. (2000). "Sexual Harassment". *Annual Review of Sex Research,* 11 cited by Margaret, A.L., Robert, E.A., Karen, L.M. (2006) in Sexual Harassers: Behaviours, *Motives and Change Over Time.* Sex Roles, 55, Page. 331-343.

Silverman, D. (1977). "Sexual Harassment: Working Women's Dilemma". *Quest: A Feminist Quarterly,* 3, pp. 15-23.

Sivaprakasan, P. and Suriakala, R., (2003). Women Employees: Status and Saisfaction. New Delhi, Kanishka Publishers.

Srinivasan, K. (1992). "Women in Banking and Professional Struggles" in Chetna Kalbagh (ed) Women's Struggle for Equality and Emancipation, New Delhi, Discovery Publishing House.

Srivastava, S.C. (2004). "Sexual Harassment of Women at Workplace: Law and Policy". *Indian Journal of Industrial Relations,* Vol. 39, No. 3, pp. 364-90.

Stambaugh, P.M. (1997). "The Power of Law and the Sexual Harassment Complaints of Women". *National Women's Studies Association Journal,* Vol. 9, pp. 23-42.

Stanko (1988). "Interpreting Social-sexual Behaviour in a Work Setting" cited by Julie Holiday Wayne, Christine M. Riordan, and Kecia M. Thomas (2001) in "Is all sexual harassment viewed the same? Mock Juror decisions in same and Cross Gender Cases". *Journal of Applied Psychology,* Vol. 86, No. 2.

Stewart, D.E. and Robinson, G.E. (1995). "Violence Against Women", cited by Hatch-Maillette, M.A., Scalora, M.J. (2002), "Gender, Sexual Harassment, Work Place Violence, and Risk Assessment: Convergence Around Psychiatric Staff's Perceptions of Personal Safety". *Journal of Aggression and Violent Behaviour*, 7, pp. 271-91.

Stockdale, M.S. (1995), "The Direct and Moderating Influences of Sexual Harassment Pervasiveness, Coping Strategies and gender on work related outcomes". *Psychology of Women Quarterly*, Vol. 22, pp. 521-35.

Summers, R.J. (1991). "Determinants of Judgements of and Responses to a Complaint of Sexual Harassment". *Sex Roles*, Vol. 25, Nos. 7-8, pp. 379-92.

Tang, C. (2000). "Report on Sexual Harassment in Workplace in China". Working paper for the ILO, Beijing.

Tangri, S.S., Burt, M.R., Johnson, L.B. (1982). "Sexual Harassment at Work: Three Explanatory Models". *Journal of Social Issues*, Vol. 28, No. 4, pp. 33-54.

Tejani, S. (2004). "Sexual Harassment at the Workplace—emerging Problems and Debates". *Economic and Political Weekly*, October 9, No. 39, pp. 4491-94.

Terpstra, D.E. and Baker, D.D. (1991). "Sexual Harassment: Psychological Issues" In M.J. Davidson and Earnshaw (eds.), Vulnerable Workers: Psycho-Social and Legal Issues, England: Wiley.

Terpstra, D.E. and Cook, S.E. (1985). "Complainant Characteristics and Reported Behaviours and Consequences Associated with Formal Sexual Harassment Charges". *Personnel Psychology*, Vol. 38, No. 3, pp. 559-74.

Thacker, R.A. (1992). "A Descriptive Study of Behavioral Responses of Sexual Harassment Targets: Implications for Control Theory". *Employee Responsibilities and Rights Journal*, Vol. 5, No. 1.

U.S. Equal Employment Opportunity Commission (1999). Sexual Harassment charges, available on www.eeoc.gov/state/harass.html

U.S. Merit Systems Protection Board (1980). "Sexual Harassment of Federal Workers : An Update", cited by Kimberly T. Schneider, Suzanne Swan, and Louise F. Fitzgerald (1997), "Job-related Psychological Effects of Sexual Harassment in the Workplace : Empirical Evidence from Two Organizations". *Journal of Applied Psychology*, Vol. 82, No. 1.

U.S. Merit Systems Protection Board (1981). "Sexual Harassment of Federal Workers : Is it a Problem?" cited by Kimberly T. Schneider, Suzanne Swan, and Louise F. Fitzgerald (1997), "Job-related Psychological Effects of Sexual Harassment in the Workplace : Empirical Evidence from Two Organizations". *Journal of Applied Psychology,* Vol. 82, No. 1.

U.S. Merits System Protection Board (1985). "Sexual Harassment in the Federal Workplace. Trends Progress and Continuing Challenges". Washington, DC: U.S. Government Printing Office cited in *Human Resource Management Review,* Vol. 10, No. 2, 2000.

U.S. Merit Systems Protection Board (1987). "Sexual Harassment of Federal Workers : An Update" cited by Kimberly T. Schneider, Suzanne Swan, and Louise F. Fitzgerald (1997). "Job-related Psychological Effects of Sexual Harassment in the Workplace : Empirical Evidence from Two Organizations". *Journal of Applied Psychology,* Vol. 82, No. 1.

U.S. Merit Systems Protection Board (1988). Sexual Harassment in the Federal Government. Washington, D.C., U.S. Government Printing Office.

U.S. Merit Systems Protection Board (1994). Sexual Harassment in the Federal Government. Washington, D.C., U.S. Government Printing Office.

Ursua, E.G. (2001). "Addressing Sexual Harassment in the Workplace: The Philippine Experience". Working Paper for the ILO, Marula.

Valentine-French, S. and Radtke, H.L. (1989). "Attributions of Responsibility for an Incident of Sexual Harassment in a University Setting". *Sex Roles,* Vol. 21, No. 7-8, pp. 545-55.

Watson, H. (1994). "Red Herrings and Mystifications: Conflicting Perceptions of Sexual Harassment" In Brant, Clare, *et. al.* (eds.). Rethinking Sexual Harassment. Boulder, Colorado, Pluto Press.

Wijayatilake, K. and Zackariya, F. (2000). "Sexual Harassment at Work—Sri Lanka Study—with Focus on the Plantation Sector". *Working Paper for the ILO,* Colombo.

Working Women United Institute (1975). "Sexual Harassment on the Job: Results of a Preliminary Survey". Ithaca, N.Y.: Author.

Workman, J.E. and Johnson, K.K.P. (1991). "The Role of Cosmetics in Attributions about Sexual Harassment". *Sex Roles*, Vol. 24, No. 11-12, pp. 759-69.

Yama Kawa, R. (2001). "Prevention and Remedies Regarding Sexual Harassment in Japan". *Working paper for the ILO*, Tsukuba.

Zaitun, M.K. (2001). "Action against Sexual Harassment in the Workplace: Asian Women's Perspective". Paper for the *ILO and the Committee for Asian Women*, Kuala Lumpur.

Index